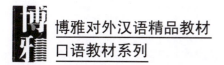
博雅对外汉语精品教材
口语教材系列

初级汉语口语(1)

(第三版)

ELEMENTARY SPOKEN CHINESE 1
(Third Edition)

词语表、课文翻译与练习参考答案

戴桂芙　刘立新　李海燕　编著

目　录

分课词语表(英日韩文注释) ··· 1
 第 四 课　你叫什么名字? ·· 1
 第 五 课　你在几班? ·· 3
 第 六 课　现在几点? ·· 5
 第 七 课　食堂在哪儿? ·· 8
 第 八 课　一共多少钱? ·· 10
 第 九 课　你有什么事? ·· 13
 第 十 课　她病了 ·· 15
 第 十一 课　我喜欢喝茶 ·· 18
 第 十二 课　你干什么呢? ·· 20
 第 十三 课　我去图书馆借书 ·· 23
 第 十四 课　今天天气怎么样? ·· 26
 第 十五 课　一个星期有多少节课? ·· 28
 第 十六 课　请问,去动物园怎么走? ······································ 31
 第 十七 课　又好吃又便宜 ·· 34
 第 十八 课　我想请你做我的辅导,好吗? ································ 37
 第 十九 课　我有点儿不舒服 ·· 39
 第 二十 课　你的爱好是什么? ·· 42
 第二十一课　八点我正在教室上课呢 ······································ 45
 第二十二课　旅行回来了 ·· 47
 第二十三课　穿什么衣服合适? ··· 50
 第二十四课　你家有什么人? ·· 52
 第二十五课　寒假打算怎么过? ··· 54

词语总表 ··· 58

量词表 ·· 73

语言点索引 ·· 77

课文英文翻译 ··· 80

练习参考答案 ··· 96

分课词语表（英日韩文注释）

第四课　你叫什么名字？

◆ 生词　New words

1. 你　　　（代）　　　nǐ　　　you
あなた、君
너, 당신

2. 叫　　　（动）　　　jiào　　　to call, to name
（名前は）〜という
부르다

3. 什么　　（代）　　　shénme　　what
何
무엇

4. 名字　　（名）　　　míngzi　　name
名前
이름

5. 好　　　（形）　　　hǎo　　　good
よい
좋다

6. 我　　　（代）　　　wǒ　　　I
わたし
나

7. 你们　　（代）　　　nǐmen　　you
あなたたち
너희

8. 姓　　　（名、动）　xìng　　　surname; family name
姓
성씨

9. 您　　　（代）　　　nín　　　a polite form of "你"
あなた（你の敬称）
당신

10. 老师　　（名）　　　lǎoshī　　teacher
先生
선생님

11. 呢　　　（助）　　　ne　　　(modal particle)
〜は？（疑問文の文末に用いる）
의문문 또는 반복 의문문의 끝에 쓰임

12. 是　　　（动）　　　shì　　　to be
〜です、〜だ
이다

13. 人　　　（名）　　　rén　　　person, people
人
사람

1

14. 我们	（代）	wǒmen	we 私たち 우리	
15. 留学生	（名）	liúxuésheng	overseas student 留学生 유학생	
16. 他	（代）	tā	he, him 彼 그 (남자)	
17. 她	（代）	tā	she, her 彼女 그 (여자)	
18. 都	（副）	dōu	all みんな、すべて 모두, 다	
19. 的	（助）	de	(structural particle) 〜の (名詞の修飾語をつくる) 의 (한정어와 중심어를 연결하는 종속을 나타 내는 수식관계)	

◆ 专名 Proper nouns

1. 杰夫		Jiéfū	Jeff ジェフ (人名) 제프 (인명)
2. 安妮		Ānnī	Annie アニー (人名) 애니 (인명)
3. 田		Tián	(a surname of a Chinese) 田 (人名) 전 (성씨)
4. 王平		Wáng Píng	(a name of a Chinese) 王平 (人名) 왕평 (인명)
5. 中国		Zhōngguó	China 中国 중국 (국명)

◆ 补充词语 Additional words

1. 大家	（名）	dàjiā	everybody, all みんな 모두
2. 学生	（名）	xuésheng	student 学生 학생
3. 张	（名）	Zhāng	(a surname of a Chinese) 張 (人名) 장 (성씨)

4. 李	（名）	Lǐ	(a surname of a Chinese) 李（人名） (성씨)	
5. 王	（名）	Wáng	(a surname of a Chinese) 王（人名） 왕씨	
6. 汉语	（名）	Hànyǔ	Chinese language 中国語 한어(중국어)	
7. 日本	（名）	Rìběn	Japan 日本 일본	

第五课　你在几班？

◆ 生词　New words

1. 在	（动、介）	zài	to be; in, at, on 〜にいる 에 있다, …에(서)
2. 几	（代）	jǐ	how many いくつ 몇 (주로 10이하의 확실하지 않은 숫자를 물어볼 때 쓰임)
3. 班	（名、量）	bān	class 班、クラス 반
4. 早上	（名）	zǎoshang	morning 朝 아침
5. 早	（形）	zǎo	early おはよう 이른 아침 인사; 안녕하세요?
6. 哪	（代）	nǎ	which, where どの、どちらの、どれ 어느
7. 国	（名）	guó	country 国 나라
8. 也	（副）	yě	too, also 〜も 도
9. 吗	（助）	ma	an interrogative particle 〜ですか？(疑問をあらわす助詞) ~까 (문장의 끝에 사용하며 의문을 표시함)

10. 不	（副）	bù	not, no いいえ 아니다
11. 谁	（代）	shuí (shéi)	who だれ 누구
12. 对	（形）	duì	yes, right, correct そのとおりだ 맞다, 옳다
13. 多大		duō dà	how old どれくらい、どれほど 몇 살
14. 十九	（数）	shíjiǔ	nineteen 19 십구, 열아홉
15. 岁	（量）	suì	year of (age) 歳、(年齢を数える量詞) 살, 세
16. 二十	（数）	èrshí	twenty 20 이십, 스물
17. 一	（数）	yī	one 1 하나
18. 二	（数）	èr	two 2 이, 둘
19. 今年	（名）	jīnnián	this year 今年 금년
20. 他们	（代）	tāmen	they 彼ら 그들

◆ 专名 Proper nouns

1. 彼得	Bǐdé	Peter ピーター（人名） 피터(인명)
2. 美国	Měiguó	USA アメリカ 미국
3. 法国	Fǎguó	France フランス 프랑스
4. 英国	Yīngguó	UK イギリス 영국

补充词语 Additional words

1.	上午	（名）	shàngwǔ	morning 午前 오전
2.	晚上	（名）	wǎnshang	evening 夜、晩、夕方 밤, 저녁
3.	下午	（名）	xiàwǔ	afternoon 午後 오후
4.	韩国	（名）	Hánguó	korea 韓国 한국
5.	德国	（名）	Déguó	Germany ドイツ 독일
6.	女	（形）	nǚ	female 女 여자
7.	男	（形）	nán	male 男 남자

第六课 现在几点？

生词 New words

1.	现在	（名）	xiànzài	now いま、現在 현재
2.	点	（量、名）	diǎn	(used to indicate time) o'clock 時（時間の単位） 점
3.	七	（数）	qī	seven 7 일곱
4.	半	（数）	bàn	half 半、2分の1 반, 절반
5.	今天	（名）	jīntiān	today 今日 오늘
6.	星期	（名）	xīngqī	week 曜日 주

5

7. 八	（数）	bā	eight 8 여덟
8. 没有	（动、副）	méiyǒu	no; have not ない（存在の否定を表す） 없다（부정을 표시함）
9. 课	（名）	kè	class, course, subject, lesson 授業 과
10. 明天	（名）	míngtiān	tomorrow 明日 내일
11. 有	（动）	yǒu	to have ある、いる 있다
12. 上课		shàng kè	to go to class 授業に出る、授業が始まる 수업을 하다
13. 上午	（名）	shàngwǔ	morning, a. m. 午前 오전
14. 从……到……		cóng……dào……	from...to... 〜から〜まで〜 로 부터…에 이르다
15. 九	（数）	jiǔ	nine 9 아홉
16. 五十	（数）	wǔshí	fifty 五十 오십, 쉰
17. 分	（量、名）	fēn	minute 分（時間の単位） 분
18. 口语	（名）	kǒuyǔ	oral language, spoken language 口語 회화
19. 差	（动）	chà	to differ from, to be short of 足りない、不足する 틀리다, 차이가 나다
20. 两	（数）	liǎng	two 2 둘
21. 该……了		gāi……le	it's time for... 〜すべきである 해야 한다
22. 再见	（动）	zàijiàn	to say goodbye さようなら 안녕

◆ 专名 Proper nouns

丽莎　　　　　　　　　　　　Lìshā　　　　　　Lisa
　　　　　　　　　　　　　　　　　　　　　　リサ（人名）
　　　　　　　　　　　　　　　　　　　　　　리사

◆ 补充词语 Additional words

1. 刻　　　（量）　　　kè　　　　quarter
　　　　　　　　　　　　　　　　15分間
　　　　　　　　　　　　　　　　15분

2. 手表　　（名）　　　shǒubiǎo　watch
　　　　　　　　　　　　　　　　時計
　　　　　　　　　　　　　　　　손목 시계

3. 钱　　　（名）　　　qián　　　money
　　　　　　　　　　　　　　　　お金
　　　　　　　　　　　　　　　　돈

4. 中文　　（名）　　　Zhōngwén　Chinese (language)
　　　　　　　　　　　　　　　　中国語
　　　　　　　　　　　　　　　　중국어

5. 时间　　（名）　　　shíjiān　　time
　　　　　　　　　　　　　　　　時間
　　　　　　　　　　　　　　　　시간

6. 听力　　（名）　　　tīnglì　　hearing, listening comprehension
　　　　　　　　　　　　　　　　（外国語の）聞き取り能力
　　　　　　　　　　　　　　　　듣기

7. 汉字　　（名）　　　Hànzì　　Chinese character
　　　　　　　　　　　　　　　　漢字
　　　　　　　　　　　　　　　　한자

8. 下课　　　　　　　　xià kè　　class is over, dismiss the class
　　　　　　　　　　　　　　　　授業が終わる
　　　　　　　　　　　　　　　　수업이 끝나다

9. 吃饭　　　　　　　　chī fàn　　have a meal
　　　　　　　　　　　　　　　　食事をする
　　　　　　　　　　　　　　　　식사를 하다

10. 起床　　　　　　　　qǐ chuáng　get up
　　　　　　　　　　　　　　　　起きる
　　　　　　　　　　　　　　　　일어나다

11. 睡觉　　　　　　　　shuì jiào　go to bed, sleep
　　　　　　　　　　　　　　　　眠る
　　　　　　　　　　　　　　　　잠자다

第七课　食堂在哪儿？

◆ 生词　New words

1. 食堂　　（名）　　shítáng　　dinning room, canteen
食堂
식당

2. 哪儿　　（代）　　nǎr　　where
どこ
어디

3. 请问　　（动）　　qǐngwèn　　may I ask..., excuse me
お尋ねします
말씀 좀 묻겠습니다

4. 三　　（数）　　sān　　three
3
셋

5. 教室　　（名）　　jiàoshì　　classroom
教室
교실

6. 这儿　　（代）　　zhèr　　here
ここ、こちら
여기(북경말)

7. 谢谢　　（动）　　xièxie　　to thank (sb)
ありがとうございます
감사하다

8. 不用　　（副）　　búyòng　　needn't
～する必要がない
필요없다

9. 学生　　（名）　　xuésheng　　student, pupil
学生、生徒
학생

10. 那儿　　（代）　　nàr　　there
あそこ、あちら
저기

11. 边　　（名）　　biān　　suffix of a noun of locality
～の側、～の方
쪽, 편

12. 宿舍　　（名）　　sùshè　　dormitory
宿舍、寮
기숙사

13. 旁边　　（名）　　pángbiān　　side, nearby
横、そば
옆쪽

14. 厕所　　（名）　　cèsuǒ　　lavatory, toilet
トイレ
변소

15.	这个		zhè ge	this この、その 이것
16.	右边	（名）	yòubian	on the right 右側 오른쪽
17.	那个		nà ge	that あれ、あちら 저것
18.	左边	（名）	zuǒbian	on the left 左側 왼쪽
19.	这	（代）	zhè (zhèi)	this これ、こちら 이
20.	学校	（名）	xuéxiào	school 学校 학교
21.	很	（副）	hěn	very とても、たいへん 매우
22.	大	（形）	dà	big 大きい 크다
23.	地方	（名）	dìfang	place ところ、場所 장소
24.	那	（代）	nà (nèi)	that あれ 저

◆ 专名 Proper nouns

1.	朴志永		Piáo Zhìyǒng	Piao Zhiyong 朴志永 박지영
2.	山田		Shāntián	Yamada 山田 야마다

◆ 补充词语 Additional words

1.	笔	（名）	bǐ	pen, pencil ペン、鉛筆 붓 혹은 필기용구
2.	书	（名）	shū	book 本 책

3. 下边	（名）	xiàbian	under, below
			下、下の方
			아래
4. 小	（形）	xiǎo	small
			小さい
			작다
5. 多	（形）	duō	more, a lot of
			多い
			많다

第八课　一共多少钱？

◆ 生 词　New words

1. 一共	（副）	yígòng	altogether
			あわせて、全部で
			전부
2. 多少	（代）	duōshao	how many
			いくら、どれほど
			얼마
3. 钱	（名）	qián	money
			お金、代金
			돈
4. 服务员	（名）	fúwùyuán	waiter/waitress
			店員
			종업원
5. 要	（助动、动）	yào	to need, to want
			欲しい（動詞），～したい（助動詞）
			원하다
6. 哪个		nǎ ge	which
			どれ、どの
			어느 것
7. 菜	（名）	cài	dish
			料理
			반찬
8. 块（元）	（量）	kuài (yuán)	(the basic unit of RMB same as "yuan")
			块（＝元）
			원(중국의 화폐 단위)
9. 毛（角）	（量）	máo (jiǎo)	(the basic unit of RMB same as "jiao")
			毛（＝角）　"一元"の１０分の１
			전(일원의 십분의 일)
10. 还	（副）	hái	too, also, as well
			さらに
			아직, 아직도, 여전히
11. 那边	（代）	nàbiān	there
			そこ、あそこ
			저쪽

12.	四	(数)	sì	four 4 넷
13.	买	(动)	mǎi	to buy 買う 사다
14.	种	(量)	zhǒng	kind, type 種類 종, 종류, 가지
15.	自行车	(名)	zìxíngchē	bike 自転車 자전거
16.	颜色	(名)	yánsè	colour 色 색깔
17.	黑	(形)	hēi	black 黒い 까만
18.	怎么样	(代)	zěnmeyàng	How about... どうですか 어떻게, 어째서, 왜
19.	喜欢	(动)	xǐhuan	to like, to be fond of 好き 좋아하다
20.	蓝色	(名)	lánsè	blue 青色 파란색
21.	车	(名)	chē	vehicle, bicycle 自転車、車 차
22.	蓝	(形)	lán	blue 青い 파란
23.	售货员	(名)	shòuhuòyuán	shop assistant, salesclerk 店員 판매원, 점원
24.	辆	(量)	liàng	(measure word for) bicycles or vehicles 台(車輪のあるものを数える) 대(자동차나 자전거를 세는 단위)
25.	百	(数)	bǎi	hundred 百 백
26.	看	(动)	kàn	to look at 見る 보다

27. 了	（助）	le	used after a verb or adjective to indicate completion of work or change 動作・行為の完了や状態の変化を表す 문장의 끝에 쓰여서 변화 또는 새로운 상황의 출현을 뜻함
28. 花	（动）	huā	to spend, to cost 払う、使う 쓰다, 소비하다

◆ 补充词语　Additional words

1. 本	（量）	běn	(measure word for) books 冊（書物などを数える） 권(책을 세는 단위)
2. 支	（量）	zhī	(measure word for) pencils/pens （筆の単位）本 자루
3. 双	（量）	shuāng	(measure word) pair 対になっているものを数える量詞 한 켤레
4. 鞋	（名）	xié	shoes 靴 신발
5. 件	（量）	jiàn	(measure word for) clothes, gift, etc. 枚、着（衣類を数える） 가지(옷을 세는 단위)
6. 衣服	（名）	yīfu	clothes 服 옷
7. 白	（形）	bái	white 白 흰
8. 面包	（名）	miànbāo	bread パン 빵
9. 喝	（动）	hē	to drink 飲む 마시다
10. 杯	（量）	bēi	(measure word for) cup, glass 杯（コップなど容器を単位として液体を数える） 컵
11. 茶	（名）	chá	tea お茶 차

第九课　你有什么事？

◆生词　New words

1. 事　　　　（名）　　shì　　　　thing, matter
   事、用事
   일

2. 作业　　　（名）　　zuòyè　　homework
   宿題
   숙제

3. 个　　　　（量）　　gè　　　　(measure word)
   個（最も広く用いられる量詞）
   개

4. 问题　　　（名）　　wèntí　　question, problem
   問題
   문제

5. 懂　　　　（动）　　dǒng　　to understand
   わかる、理解する
   이해하다

6. 问　　　　（动）　　wèn　　to ask
   聞く、たずねる
   물어보다

7. 吧　　　　（助）　　ba　　　　(modal particle)
   文末につけて相談・要求の意を表す
   문장의 끝에 쓰여 제의를 나타냄

8. 知道　　　（动）　　zhīdào　　to know, to realise
   知っている
   알다

9. 电话　　　（名）　　diànhuà　telephone
   電話
   전화

10. 号码　　　（名）　　hàomǎ　　number
    番号
    번호

11. 办公室　　（名）　　bàngōngshì　office
    事務室
    사무실

12. 六　　　　（数）　　liù　　　　six
    6
    여섯

13. 零（〇）　（数）　　líng　　　zero
    ゼロ
    영

14. 给　　　　（介、动）　gěi　　　to, for; to give
    〜に（介詞）・あげる（動詞）
    에게, 주다

15. 打(电话)	(动)	dǎ	to make (a phone call) (電話を)する (전화를)걸다
16. 喂	(叹)	wèi	hello もしもし 여보세요
17. 晚上	(名)	wǎnshang	evening 夜 저녁
18. 时间	(名)	shíjiān	time 時間 시간
19. 生日	(名)	shēngrì	birthday 誕生日 생일
20. 一起	(副)	yīqǐ	together 一緒に 같이
21. 玩儿	(动)	wánr	to play, to have fun 遊ぶ 놀다
22. 住	(动)	zhù	to live, to reside, to stay 住む 살다
23. 号	(量、名)	hào	number 号 번호를 매길 때 쓰는 단위
24. 楼	(名)	lóu	storied building 建物、棟 동
25. 说	(动)	shuō	to speak, to say 言う、話す 말하다
26. 件	(量)	jiàn	(measure word for) clothes, gift, etc. (総称を表す名詞を数える) 가지 (사물을 세는 단위)
27. 礼物	(名)	lǐwù	gift, present プレゼント 선물
28. 祝	(动)	zhù	to express good wishes 祝う 축하하다
29. 快乐	(形)	kuàilè	happy, joy 楽しい 즐겁다

补充词语　Additional words

1. 等　　　（动）　　děng　　　to wait
　　　　　　　　　　　　　　　　待つ
　　　　　　　　　　　　　　　　기다리다

2. 房间　　（名）　　fángjiān　　room
　　　　　　　　　　　　　　　　部屋
　　　　　　　　　　　　　　　　방

3. 月　　　（名）　　yuè　　　　month
　　　　　　　　　　　　　　　　月（がつ）
　　　　　　　　　　　　　　　　월

4. 昨天　　（名）　　zuótiān　　yesterday
　　　　　　　　　　　　　　　　昨日
　　　　　　　　　　　　　　　　어제

5. 真　　　（副）　　zhēn　　　really
　　　　　　　　　　　　　　　　本当に
　　　　　　　　　　　　　　　　정말

6. 忙　　　（形）　　máng　　　busy
　　　　　　　　　　　　　　　　忙しい
　　　　　　　　　　　　　　　　바쁘다

7. 想　　　（动）　　xiǎng　　　to think, to want to, to suppose
　　　　　　　　　　　　　　　　考える；…したい；…するつもりです
　　　　　　　　　　　　　　　　생각하다

8. 饭馆儿　（名）　　fànguǎnr　restaurant
　　　　　　　　　　　　　　　　レストラン、ホテル
　　　　　　　　　　　　　　　　식당

9. 去　　　（动）　　qù　　　　to go to
　　　　　　　　　　　　　　　　行く
　　　　　　　　　　　　　　　　가다

10. 商场　　（名）　　shāngchǎng　emporium, marketplace
　　　　　　　　　　　　　　　　デパート
　　　　　　　　　　　　　　　　쇼핑 센터

11. 打算　　（动、名）　dǎsuan　intend
　　　　　　　　　　　　　　　　するつもりである
　　　　　　　　　　　　　　　　~할 계획이다, 계획

12. 朋友　　（名）　　péngyou　friend
　　　　　　　　　　　　　　　　友達
　　　　　　　　　　　　　　　　친구

第十课　她病了

生词　New words

1. 病　　　（动、名）　bìng　　to be sick; sickness
　　　　　　　　　　　　　　　　病気になる・病気
　　　　　　　　　　　　　　　　병나다, 병

2. 怎么	（代）	zěnme	why, how どうしましたか（状況を問う） 어떻게
3. 头	（名）	tóu	head 頭 머리
4. 疼	（形）	téng	achy, painful 痛い 아프다
5. 感冒	（动、名）	gǎnmào	to have a cold; a flu 風邪を引く・風邪 감기에 걸리다, 감기
6. 想	（助动、动）	xiǎng	to want to, to think; to miss ～したい 생각하다
7. 回	（动）	huí	to return to, to go back 帰る、戻る 돌아가다, 돌아오다
8. 房间	（名）	fángjiān	room 部屋 방
9. 休息	（动）	xiūxi	to have a rest 休む 쉬다
10. 告诉	（动）	gàosu	to tell 伝える 말하다
11. 能	（助动）	néng	can できる 할수있다
12. 来	（动）	lái	to come 来る 오다
13. 请	（动）	qǐng	to please, to invite どうぞ（～してください）、頼む 요청하다, 부탁하다
14. 进	（动）	jìn	to go into 入る 들어가다
15. 对不起	（动）	duìbuqǐ	sorry, excuse me すみません 미안하다
16. 晚	（形）	wǎn	late, to be late おそい、遅れる 늦다
17. 才	（副）	cái	then and only then やっと、ようやく 이제야

18. 闹钟	（名）	nàozhōng	alarm clock 目覚まし時計 괘종시계
19. 睡觉		shuì jiào	sleep 眠る 잠자다
20. 刻	（量）	kè	quarter （一刻で）15分、（三刻で）45分 15분
21. 起床		qǐ chuáng	to get up 起きる 일어나다
22. 所以	（连）	suǒyǐ	so, therefore, as a result だから 그래서, 그러므로
23. 停	（动）	tíng	to stop 止まる 멎다, 서다
24. 去	（动）	qù	to go to 行く 가다
25. 大使馆	（名）	dàshǐguǎn	embassy 大使館 대사관
26. 请假		qǐng jià	to ask for leave 休暇をもらう 휴가를 신청하다
27. 天	（名）	tiān	day 日 날

◆ 补充词语　Additional words

1. 肚子	（名）	dùzi	stomach おなか 배
2. 嗓子	（名）	sǎngzi	throat のど 목(구멍)
3. 牙	（名）	yá	teeth 歯 이빨
4. 腿	（名）	tuǐ	leg 足 다리
5. 手	（名）	shǒu	hand 手 손

6. 没	（动、副）	méi	not have, no, not 持っていない．ない．存在しない 없다
7. 迟到	（动）	chídào	to be late 遅刻する 늦다
8. 慢	（形）	màn	slow 遅れてる 느리다

第十一课　我喜欢喝茶

◆ 生 词　New words

1. 喝	（动）	hē	to drink 飲む 마시다
2. 茶	（名）	chá	tea お茶 차
3. 吃	（动）	chī	to eat 食べる 먹다
4. 馒头	（名）	mántou	steamed bread 中国式蒸しパン 찐빵(속을 넣지 않은 것)
5. 饺子	（名）	jiǎozi	dumpling ぎょうざ 물만두
6. 斤	（量）	jīn	half a kilo 500グラム 근
7. 大概	（副、形）	dàgài	most likely; rough たぶん、おそらく 대개
8. 完	（动）	wán	to be finished, to be over 〜してしまう、なくなる 끝나다
9. 没	（动、副）	méi	not have, no, not 持っていない．ない．存在しない 없다
10. 好吃	（形）	hǎochī	delicious おいしい 맛있다
11. 葡萄	（名）	pútao	grape 葡萄 포도

18

12. 酸	（形）	suān	sour すっぱい 시다
13. 甜	（形）	tián	sweet 甘い 달다
14. 可以	（助动）	kěyǐ	can, may 〜してもいい 할 수 있다
15. 尝	（动）	cháng	to have a taste of 味わってみる 맛보다
16. 便宜	（形）	piányi	not expensive, cheap 安い 싸다
17. 一点儿	（数量）	yìdiǎnr	a bit, a little 少し 조금
18. 讲价		jiǎng jià	to bargain 値段を掛け合う 값을 흥정하다
19. 欢迎	（动）	huānyíng	to welcome 歓迎する 환영하다
20. 坐	（动）	zuò	to sit 座る 앉다
21. 还是	（连、副）	háishi	or; still それとも 아니면
22. 咖啡	（名）	kāfēi	coffee コーヒー 커피
23. 以前	（名）	yǐqián	before, in the past; ago 以前 그전
24. 桌子	（名）	zhuōzi	table 机、テーブル 테이블
25. 上边	（名）	shàngbian	over, on top 上 위쪽
26. 点心	（名）	diǎnxin	light refreshments お菓子、軽食 간식
27. 随便	（形）	suíbiàn	random, as one please 自由に、気軽に 마음대로 하다

| 28. 以后 | （名） | yǐhòu | after, in the future
以後、～の後
나중 |
| 29. 习惯 | （动、名） | xíguàn | to be used to; habit
慣れる・習慣
익숙하게 되다, 습관 |

◆ 补充词语　Additional words

1. 东西	（名）	dōngxi	things 物 물건
2. 白酒	（名）	báijiǔ	white spirit 白酒（バイチユ）蒸留酒の総称 소주
3. 写	（动）	xiě	to write 書く 쓰다
4. 帮	（动）	bāng	to help 助ける、手伝う 돕다
5. 橘子	（名）	júzi	mandarin orange ミカン 귤

第十二课　你干什么呢？

◆ 生词　New words

1. 干	（动）	gàn	to do する、やる 하다
2. 门	（名）	mén	door ドア 문
3. 开	（动）	kāi	to open, to turn on 開ける. 開く. 열다
4. 着	（助）	zhe	(particle, indicating an action in progress) ～している・～しながら（～する） 하고있다
5. 好像	（副）	hǎoxiàng	seem, to be like ～みたいだ、～の気がする 한 것 같다
6. 不太	（副）	bútài	not very much あまり～でない 그다지 …하지 않다

7. 高兴	(形)	gāoxìng	glad, pleased うれしい、機嫌がよい 기쁘다
8. 有(一)点儿	(副)	yǒu (yì) diǎnr	slightly (most used for a unhappy event) すこし、どうも（望ましくないことが多い） 야묵 조금
9. 想	(动)	xiǎng	to miss 考える、思い出す 생각하다
10. 家	(名)	jiā	home, family 家、家庭 집
11. 听	(动)	tīng	to listen 聞く 듣다
12. 一会儿	(数量)	yíhuìr	a little while 少しの間、しばらく 잠깐
13. 音乐	(名)	yīnyuè	music 音楽 음악
14. 咱们	(代)	zánmen	we (including both the speaker and the listener) 私たち 상대방을 포함한 우리
15. 聊天儿		liáo tiānr	to chat おしゃべりをする、雑談をする 한담하다, 잡답하다
16. 啊	(助)	a	(modal particle) 文末に用いて疑問の語気を表す 놀람이나 캐어물음을 나타냄
17. 进来		jìnlái	to come in 入ってくる 들어오다
18. 做	(动)	zuò	to do する 하다
19. 听写	(动、名)	tīngxiě	to dictate; dictation 書き取り 듣고 쓰다
20. 生词	(名)	shēngcí	new words 新出単語 새로운 단어
21. 当然	(形)	dāngrán	naturally, without doubt もちろん、当たり前だ 당연하다

22.	真	（形）	zhēn	real, indeed 本当に 진실하다
23.	回答	（动）	huídá	to answer, to reply 答える 대답하다
24.	昨天	（名）	zuótiān	yesterday 昨日 어제
25.	星期天	（名）	xīngqītiān	sunday 日曜日 일요일
26.	为什么		wèi shénme	why なぜ、どうして 왜
27.	朋友	（名）	péngyou	friend 友達 친구
28.	可是	（连）	kěshì	but しかし、でも 그러나
29.	觉得	（动）	juéde	to feel, to think 〜と思う 느끼다

◆ 补充词语　Additional words

1.	贵	（形）	guì	expensive 高い 비싸다
2.	苹果	（名）	píngguǒ	apple りんご 사과
3.	电视	（名）	diànshì	television テレビ 텔레비죤
4.	篮球	（名）	lánqiú	basketball バスケット・ボール 농구
5.	歌	（名）	gē	song 歌 노래
6.	关	（动）	guān	to close, to turn off 閉める，閉じる． 닫다
7.	戴	（动）	dài	to wear （眼鏡を）かける 착용하다, 쓰다

8. 眼镜	（名）	yǎnjìng	glasses 眼鏡 안경
9. 瓶	（名、量）	píng	bottle; a measure word 本（ビンに入っているものを数える） 병
10. 酒	（名）	jiǔ	wine 酒 술
11. 这些	（代）	zhèxiē	those; these これら 이런 것들

第十三课　我去图书馆借书

◆ 生词　New words

1. 图书馆	（名）	túshūguǎn	library 図書館 도서관
2. 借	（动）	jiè	to borrow 借りる 빌리다
3. 书	（名）	shū	book 本 책
4. 本	（量）	běn	(measure word for) books, etc. 冊 권
5. 要是	（连）	yàoshi	if then もし．もしも…なら 만약, 만약~라면
6. 和	（连、介）	hé	and; with ～と 와
7. 关	（动）	guān	to close 閉まる 닫다
8. 不过	（连）	búguò	but しかし．でも 그러나, 그런데
9. 自习	（动）	zìxí	self-study 自習(する) 자습하다, 자습
10. 着急		zháo jí	worried イライラする．心配する 조급해하다

23

11. 网	(名)	wǎng	network ネットワーク 그물
12. 上(网)	(动)	shàng (wǎng)	to surf the internet インターネットをする 인터넷을 하다
13. 方便	(形)	fāngbiàn	convenient 便利 편리하다
14. 价钱	(名)	jiàqián	price 値段 가격, 값
15. 帮	(动)	bāng	to help 助ける．手伝う 돕다
16. 下(订单)	(动)	xià (dìngdān)	to place (an order) 注文する 주문하다
17. 订单	(名)	dìngdān	order 注文 주문서, 주문 명세서
18. 送	(动)	sòng	to deliver 届ける 보내다
19. 快	(形)	kuài	quick 速い 빠르다
20. 寄	(动)	jì	to post 郵送する、だす 부치다, 보내다
21. 快递	(名)	kuàidì	express delivery 速達 특급 우편, 택배
22. 填	(动)	tián	to fill in 書き入れる 써 넣다, 기입하다
23. 一下	(数量)	yíxià	one time, once ちょっと…する 단시간에
24. 单	(名)	dān	form 表 혼자, 하나
25. 对方	(名)	duìfāng	the other party 相手 상대방
26. 付款		fù kuǎn	to pay お金を払う 돈을 지불하다

27. 找(钱)	(动)	zhǎo(qián)	to give (sb.) (change) つり銭を出す 찾다	
28. 刚才	(名)	gāngcái	just now さっき 금방	
29. 收	(动)	shōu	to receive 受け取る. 手に入る. 받다	

◆ **专名　Proper nouns**

1. 英文	(名)	Yīngwén	English 英語 영어, 영문
2. 上海		Shànghǎi	Shanghai 上海 상하이, 상해
3. 西安		Xī'ān	Xi'an 西安 시안, 서안

◆ **补充词语　Additional words**

1. 旅行	(动)	lǚxíng	travel 旅行 여행하다, 여행
2. 话	(名)	huà	word, talk 言葉. 話. 言語. 말
3. 发	(动)	fā	to send 送信する. 보내다
4. 先生	(名)	xiānsheng	mister さん. 様 선생님, 씨(성인 남성에 대한 경칭)
5. 错	(形)	cuò	wrong 正しくない. 틀리다
6. 用	(动)	yòng	to use 使う 사용하다
7. 电脑	(名)	diànnǎo	computer コンピューター 컴퓨터
8. 手机	(名)	shǒujī	cellphone 携帯电话 핸드폰

9. 常常	（副）	cháng cháng		often いつも 자주
10. 地址	（名）	dìzhǐ		address あて先. 주소

第十四课　今天天气怎么样？

◆ 生词　New words

1. 天气	（名）	tiānqì		weather 天気、気候 날씨
2. 不错	（形）	búcuò		good, not bad よい、すばらしい 맞다
3. 热	（形）	rè		hot 暑い 덥다
4. 夜里	（名）	yèli		midnight 夜 밤중
5. 下(雨)	（动）	xià (yǔ)		to rain （雨が）降る (yǔ)(비가) 오다
6. 小	（形）	xiǎo		small 小さい 작은
7. 雨	（名）	yǔ		rain 雨 비
8. 风	（名）	fēng		wind 風 바람
9. 冬天	（名）	dōngtiān		winter 冬 겨울
10. 冷	（形）	lěng		cold 寒い 춥다
11. 非常	（副）	fēicháng		very 大変、非常に 매우
12. 夏天	（名）	xiàtiān		summer 夏 여름

13. 特别	(副、形)	tèbié	particularly; especially, special とりわけ、特に 특별하다
14. 春天	(名)	chūntiān	spring 春 봄
15. 秋天	(名)	qiūtiān	autumn, fall 秋 가을
16. 季节	(名)	jìjié	season 季節 계절
17. 阿姨	(名)	āyí	auntie (form of address for a woman of one's parents' generation but not related to one's family) おばさん、おねえさん 아주머니
18. 听说	(动)	tīngshuō	It is said that, to be told that 聞くところによると〜だ 듣기로는, 듣건데
19. 身体	(名)	shēntǐ	body, health 体 몸
20. 已经	(副)	yǐjīng	already すでに 벌써
21. 最近	(名)	zuìjìn	recently 最近 최근
22. 学习	(动)	xuéxí	to study, to learn 勉強、勉強する 공부하다
23. 忙	(形)	máng	busy 忙しい 바쁘다
24. 饭	(名)	fàn	meal 食事 밥
25. 还可以		hái kěyǐ	it's OK, it's not bad まぁまぁである、そう悪くない 괜찮다
26. 妈妈	(名)	māma	mother お母さん 엄마
27. 让	(动)	ràng	to let 〜させる 하도록 시키다

28. 放心		fàng xīn	feel safe, be at ease 安心する 안심하다

◆ 专名　Proper nouns

李文静		Lǐ Wénjìng	(a name of a Chinese) 李文静(人名) 이문정(인영)

◆ 补充词语　Additional words

1. 大衣	（名）	dàyī	overcoat コート、オーバー 외투
2. 咖啡馆儿	（名）	kāfēiguǎnr	coffee bar; café 喫茶店 커피숍
3. 孩子	（名）	háizi	child(ren), kid(s) 子供 아이,어린이
4. 生活	（名、动）	shēnghuó	life; to live 生活 생활

第十五课　一个星期有多少节课？

◆ 生词　New words

1. 节	（量、名）	jié	(measure word for) lesson; festival こま（区切りに分けられるものを数える） 째
2. 时候	（名）	shíhou	time 時、時間 시간, 때
3. 放(假)	（动）	fàng (jià)	to have (a vacation) 休暇になる、休みになる 휴가로 쉬다,방학하다
4. 寒假	（名）	hánjià	winter vacation 冬休み 월
5. 一月	（名）	yīyuè	January 1月 겨울방학
6. 期末	（名）	qīmò	the end of the term 期末 학기말

7. 考试	（动）	kǎoshì	to examine テスト、試験 시험, 시험보다	
8. 开学		kāi xué	school begins 学校が始まる 학기를 시작하다	
9. 过	（助）	guo	(a particle, used as a grammatical suffix to indicate experience) 〜したことがある 적이 있다	
10. 多	（代）	duō	how (many), how (long) どれくらい、どれほど 많다	
11. 长	（形）	cháng	long 長い、長さ 길다	
12. 月	（名）	yuè	month 月 월, 달	
13. 学期	（名）	xuéqī	semester, term 学期 학기	
14. 门	（量）	mén	(measure word for) courses 科目（学科、技術を数える） 과(목)	
15. 语法	（名）	yǔfǎ	grammar 文法 문법	
16. 听力	（名）	tīnglì	hearing 聞き取り能力 듣기	
17. 每	（代）	měi	each, every それぞれ、すべて 매	
18. 汉字	（名）	Hànzì	Chinese character 漢字 한가	
19. 下午	（名）	xiàwǔ	afternoon 午後 오후	
20. 太	（副）	tài	too すごく、大変 너무	
21. 多	（形）	duō	many, more 多い 많다	

22.	少	(形)	shǎo	little, less 少ない 적다
23.	只	(副)	zhǐ	only 〜だけ 오직
24.	学年	(名)	xuénián	school year 学年 학년
25.	第	(头)	dì	(prefix for ordinal numbers) 第 제
26.	年	(名)	nián	year 年 년
27.	周	(名)	zhōu	week 週、週間 주
28.	暑假	(名)	shǔjià	summer vacation 夏休み 여름방학

◆ 专名　Proper nouns

1.	圣诞节	Shèngdàn Jié	Christmas クリスマス 성탄절

◆ 补充词语　Additional words

1.	回国		huí guó	to return to home country 帰国する 귀국하다
2.	结婚		jié hūn	to get married 結婚する 결혼하다
3.	烤鸭	(名)	kǎoyā	roast duck アヒルの丸焼き 구운 오리고기
4.	电影	(名)	diànyǐng	movie 映画 영화
5.	书法	(名)	shūfǎ	calligraphy 書道 서예
6.	北京		Běijīng	Beijing 北京(地名) 북경

7. 长城		Chángchéng	the Great Wall 長城、万里の長城 만리장성
8. 飞机	（名）	fēijī	airplane 飛行機 비행기
9. 万	（数）	wàn	ten thousand 万 만
10. 次	（量）	cì	number of (times) 回,度,遍. 번
11. 国家	（名）	guójiā	country, nation 国、国家 국가
12. 一样	（形）	yíyàng	same 同じだ 같다
13. 中学	（名）	zhōngxué	middle school 中学、高校 중 고등학교

第十六课　请问,去动物园怎么走?

◆ 生词　New words

1. 动物园	（名）	dòngwùyuán	zoo 動物園 동물원
2. 走	（动）	zǒu	to walk 行く 가다
3. 卖	（动）	mài	to sell 買う 사다
4. 鞋	（名）	xié	shoes 靴 신발
5. 楼	（名、量）	lóu	a storied building; (measure word for) floor 階(建物の階数を数える) 동
6. 先生	（名）	xiānsheng	sir 見知らぬ男の人に対する呼び方 선생님, 씨(성인 남성에 대한 경칭)
7. 路人	（名）	lùrén	passerby 道行く人 행인

8.	往	（介）	wǎng	toward, to 〜に向けて、〜のほうへ 쪽으로
9.	前	（名）	qián	front, ahead 前 앞
10.	马路	（名）	mǎlù	road, street 大通り、自動車道路 한길, 큰길
11.	远	（形）	yuǎn	far, distant 遠い 멀다
12.	分钟	（量）	fēnzhōng	minute 分 분(간)
13.	到	（动）	dào	to arrive in/at, to get to a place 到着する 도착하다
14.	不客气		bú kèqi	you are welcome どういたしまして 천만에요
15.	同学	（名）	tóngxué	classmate クラスメート(学生に対する呼びかけ) 동창, 학우
16.	牙	（名）	yá	tooth 歯 이빨
17.	(牙)科	（名）	(yá) kē	(department of) dentistry 科(学術などの) 과
18.	清楚	（形）	qīngchu	clear よく知っている 분명하다
19.	再	（副）	zài	again, once more もう一度、再び 다시
20.	别人	（代）	biéren	other people 別の人 다른 사람
21.	大夫	（名）	dàifu	doctor 医者 의사
22.	右	（名）	yòu	right, right side 右 오른쪽
23.	拐	（动）	guǎi	to turn (角を)曲がる 돌다

24.	下课		xià kè	dismiss the class; class is over 授業が終わる 수업이 끝나다
25.	医院	（名）	yīyuàn	hospital 病院 병원
26.	层	（量）	céng	(measure word for) floor; storey 階（重なっているものを数える） 층
27.	上(楼)	（动）	shàng (lóu)	to go (upstairs) 上がる (윗층으로) 올라가다

◆ 补充词语　Additional words

1.	词典	（名）	cídiǎn	dictionary 辞書 사전
2.	茶叶	（名）	cháyè	tea leaves 茶、茶の葉 차 잎
3.	餐厅	（名）	cāntīng	dinning hall; eating room 食堂、レストラン 식당
4.	书店	（名）	shūdiàn	bookstore; bookshop 書店 책방
5.	明白	（形）	míngbai	to understand 分かる 명백하다, 분명하다
6.	认识	（动）	rènshi	to know; to recognize 見知る 알다
7.	前边	（名）	qiánbian	in front of 前方 앞쪽
8.	银行	（名）	yínháng	bank 銀行 은행
9.	东	（名）	dōng	east 東 동
10.	左	（名）	zuǒ	left 左 왼쪽
11.	西	（名）	xī	west 西 서

12. 南	（名）	nán	south
			南
			남
13. 近	（形）	jìn	near, close to
			近い
			가깝다
14. 路口	（名）	lùkǒu	crossing, intersection
			交差点；辻

第十七课　又好吃又便宜

◆ 生词　New words

1. 又……又……		yòu……yòu……	(indicating the simultaneous existence of several actions, conditions or characteristics)
			(〜でもあり) また (〜でもある)
			…하고도…하다
2. 光临	（动）	guānglín	(honorific) to attend
			ご来訪
			광림하시다 (남이 찾아오는 일을 높여 이르는 말)
3. 位	（量）	wèi	(measure word for) people
			敬意をもって人を数える.
			분
4. 里面	（名）	lǐmian	interior, inside
			中．内側．
			안, 속, 내부
5. 辣	（形）	là	hot, peppery
			辛い
			맵다
6. 点(菜)	（动）	diǎn (cài)	to order
			注文する、指定する
			주문하다
7. 菜单	（名）	càidān	menu
			メニュー
			메뉴
8. 鱼	（名）	yú	fish
			魚
			물고기
9. 茄子	（名）	qiézi	eggplant
			ナスビ
			가지
10. 别	（副）	bié	don't
			…してはいけない
			〜하지마라
11. 担心		dān xīn	to worry
			心配する
			걱정하다

12. 味道	（名）	wèidào	taste 味 맛	
13. 肉	（名）	ròu	meat 肉 고기	
14. 够	（动、副）	gòu	to reach; enough 足りる 충분하다	
15. 碗	（量、名）	wǎn	(measure word for) bowl 碗 그릇	
16. 米饭	（名）	mǐfàn	cooked rice 米の飯 쌀밥	
17. 瓶	（量、名）	píng	(measure word for) bottle 瓶（ビンに入っているのもを数える） 병	
18. 啤酒	（名）	píjiǔ	beer ビール 맥주	
19. 饿	（形）	è	hungry おなかがすく 배고프다	
20. 马上	（副）	mǎshàng	at once, immediately, right away すぐ 곧, 바로, 즉시	
21. 饭馆儿	（名）	fànguǎnr	restaurant レストラン 식당	
22. 比	（介）	bǐ	(indicating difference in manner or degree by comparison) 〜に比べて 보다	
23. 香	（形）	xiāng	delicious おいしい 맛있다	
24. 饱	（形）	bǎo	be full おなかがいっぱいになる 배부르다	
25. 打包		dǎ bāo	to take out (the food) テイクアウト、お持ち帰り 싸다	
26. 结账		jié zhàng	to settle/square accounts お勘定、お会計 계산하다	

◆ 菜名 Dish name

1. 糖醋鱼　　　　　　tángcùyú　　　　　fish in sweet and sour sauce
   魚の甘酢あんかけ
   물고기로 만든 탕수 요리

2. 西红柿炒鸡蛋　　　xīhóngshì chǎojīdàn　stir-fried egg and tomato
   トマトと玉子の炒め物
   토마토 달걀 볶음

3. 鱼香茄子　　　　　yúxiāng qiézi　　　fish-flavoured shredded pork
   ナスの炒め物（魚香風味）
   물고기 맛을 낸 가지 볶음

4. 铁板牛肉　　　　　tiěbǎn niúròu　　　sizzling beef on hot plate
   牛肉鉄板焼き
   철판 소고기 볶음

5. 炒土豆丝　　　　　chǎotǔdòusī　　　stir-fried sliced potato
   ジャガイモ千切りいため
   감자 볶음

◆ 补充词语 Additional words

1. 本子　　（名）　　běnzi　　notebook
   ノート、書物
   공책

2. 椅子　　（名）　　yǐzi　　chair
   椅子
   의자

3. 床　　　（名）　　chuáng　　bed
   ベット
   침대

4. 牛奶　　（名）　　niúnǎi　　milk
   牛乳
   우유

5. 冰激凌　（名）　　bīngjīlíng　　icecream
   アイスクリーム
   아이스크림

6. 汤　　　（名）　　tāng　　soup
   スープ
   국

7. 难　　　（形）　　nán　　hard, difficult
   難しい
   어렵다

8. 面条儿　（名）　　miàntiáor　　noodles
   めん類、うどん
   국수

9. 会　　　（动、助动）　　huì　　can; be able to
   できる
   할 수 있다

第十八课　我想请你做我的辅导，好吗？

◆ 生 词　New words

1. 辅导　　　（动）　　　fǔdǎo　　　to instruct
   補習・学習を助け指導する
   과외 지도

2. 练习　　　（动、名）　liànxí　　　to practise; exercise
   練習する・練習
   연습하다

3. 次　　　　（量）　　　cì　　　　　(measure word) time(s)
   回
   번

4. 小时　　　（名）　　　xiǎoshí　　hour
   時間(時間の単位)
   시간

5. 行　　　　（动、形）　xíng　　　　to be alright; it's okay
   よろしい、かまわない
   괜찮다

6. 这样　　　（代）　　　zhèyàng　　so, this way
   このように
   이렇게

7. 互相　　　（副）　　　hùxiāng　　each other
   お互いに
   서로

8. 水平　　　（名）　　　shuǐpíng　　standard, level
   レベル
   수평

9. 声调　　　（名）　　　shēngdiào　tone
   声調
   성조

10. 希望　　（动、名）　xīwàng　　　to hope; expectation
    〜したいと思う、希望する・希望
    희망하다

11. 地　　　（助）　　　de　　　　　(a structural particle)
    他の語句の後につけて動詞形容詞の修飾語を作る
    게, …적으로

12. 答应　　（动）　　　dāying　　　to agree, to promise
    承知する
    대답하다

13. 从　　　（介）　　　cóng　　　　from
    〜から
    …부터

14. 下　　　（名）　　　xià　　　　　next, under, within
    次の
    다음

37

15.	开始	（动）	kāishǐ	to begin, to start はじめる 시작하다
16.	教	（动）	jiāo	to teach 教える 가르치다
17.	找	（动）	zhǎo	to look for 探す．求める．見つける． 찾다
18.	手机	（名）	shǒujī	cellphone 携帯電話 핸드폰
19.	见	（动）	jiàn	to meet 会う 보다, 만나다
20.	得	（助）	de	(a structural particle) 結果・程度を表す補語を導く 동사뒤에 쓰여 정도를 나타냄
21.	挺	（副）	tǐng	very, rather とても 꽤
22.	聊	（动）	liáo	to chat 雑談する 한담하다
23.	爱好	（名）	àihào	hobby, interest 趣味 취미
24.	旅行	（动）	lǚxíng	to travel 旅行 여행
25.	专业	（名）	zhuānyè	speciality, field of study 専攻学科 전공
26.	一定	（副、形）	yídìng	surely; definite きっと 꼭
27.	有意思		yǒu yìsi	interesting おもしろい 재미있다
28.	参加	（动）	cānjiā	to take part in, participate in 参加する、加わる 참가하다

◆ 专名 Proper nouns

1.	汉语	（名）	Hànyǔ	Chinese language 中国語 한어; 궁국어

2. 英语　　　（名）　　　Yīngyǔ　　　English
英語
영어

◆ 补充词语　Additional words

1. 帮忙　　　　　　　　bāng máng　　to help
手伝う、助ける
돕다

2. 认真　　　（形）　　rènzhēn　　　conscientious, serious
まじめである、真剣である
열심이다

3. 唱　　　　（动）　　chàng　　　　to sing
歌う
오래하다

4. 首　　　　（量）　　shǒu　　　　（measure word）
曲（詩や歌を数える）
곡

5. 厉害　　　（形）　　lìhai　　　　sharp; severe
ひどい、激しい
심하다

6. 后天　　　（名）　　hòutiān　　　the day after tomorrow
明後日
내일 모레

7. 坏　　　　（形）　　huài　　　　bad; be not working properly
壊れる
고장나다

8. 商量　　　（动）　　shāngliang　　to discuss
相談する
의논하다

9. 方法　　　（名）　　fāngfǎ　　　method
方法
방법

第十九课　我有点儿不舒服

◆ 生　词　New words

1. 舒服　　　（形）　　shūfu　　　　comfortable
気分がよい、体調がよい
편안하다, 쾌적하다

2. 厉害　　　（形）　　lìhai　　　　terrible, devastating
ひどい、はげしい
심하다

3. 发烧　　　　　　　　fā shāo　　　to get a fever
熱が出る
열나다

4. 回去		huíqù	to return to, to go back かえる、戻る 돌아가다
5. 好好儿	（副）	hǎohāor	well, all out よく、ちゃんと、十分に 잘
6. 水	（名）	shuǐ	water 水 물
7. 上	（名）	shàng	previous, last 前の、先の 앞의, 지난(번)
8. 考	（动）	kǎo	to test, to exam 試験する、(試験を)受ける 시험보다
9. 准备	（动）	zhǔnbèi	to prepare 準備する 준비하다
10. 没关系		méi guānxi	It doesn't matter 大丈夫だ、心配ない 괜찮다
11. 咳嗽	（动）	késou	to cough せきをする 기침
12. 努力	（动、形）	nǔlì	to try hard; hard 努力する 노력하다
13. 关心	（动）	guānxīn	to care for, to be concerned about 関心を持つ、気にかける 관심하다
14. 得	（动）	dé	to gain, to obtain 得る 얻다
15. 重	（形）	zhòng	heavy 重い 무겁다
16. ……极了		……jíle	extremely とても、実に 아주, 극히
17. 陪	（动）	péi	to accompany お供をする、付き添う 동반하다
18. 出去		chūqù	to go out 出る、出て行く 나가다
19. 散步		sàn bù	to take a walk 散歩する 산보하다

20.	等	(动)	děng	to wait 待つ 기다리다
21.	这么	(代)	zhème	so, such, like this (indicating nature, state, way, degree, ect.) このように、こんなに 이처럼
22.	男	(形)	nán	male 男 남자 친구
23.	开玩笑		kāi wánxiào	to make fun of 冗談を言う 농담하다
24.	那	(连)	nà	then, in that case それでは 그러면
25.	先	(副、名)	xiān	earlier; first 先に 먼저
26.	改天	(副)	gǎitiān	on some other day いずれまた、あらためて 날을 바꾸다
27.	送	(动)	sòng	to deliver, to see sb off 送る、見送る 전송하다
28.	慢	(形)	màn	slow ゆっくり 느리다

◆ 专名　Proper nouns

张新		Zhāng Xīn	(a name of a Chinese) 張新(人名) 장신(인명)

◆ 补充词语　Additional words

1.	哭	(动)	kū	to cry なく 울다
2.	帮助	(动)	bāngzhù	to help 助け、援助 돕다
3.	漂亮	(形)	piàoliang	pretty, beautiful きれい．美しい 예쁘다
4.	词	(名)	cí	words 単語、語句 단어

5. 姐姐	（名）	jiějie	elder sister 姉 언니
6. 妹妹	（名）	mèimei	younger sister 妹 여동생
7. 高	（形）	gāo	tall 高い 크다
8. 站	（动）	zhàn	to stand 立つ 해보다
9. 试	（动）	shì	to try 試す 해보다
10. 骑	（动）	qí	to ride 乗る 타다
11. 修理	（动）	xiūlǐ	to repair 修理する 수리하다
12. 复习	（动）	fùxí	to review 復習する 복습하다

第二十课　你的爱好是什么？

◆ 生词　New words

1. 一般	（形）	yìbān	ordinary, average ふつう、一般である 일반적
2. 啦	（助）	la	(interj.) 事柄を列挙するときに用いる (할)랴
3. 录音		lù yīn	recording 録音（されたもの） 녹음
4. 复习	（动）	fùxí	to review 復習する 복습하다
5. 旧	（形）	jiù	old 古い、前の 지난, 옛날의
6. 预习	（动）	yùxí	to preview 予習する 예습하다

7. 新	(形)	xīn	new 新しい 새로운	
8. 真	(副)	zhēn	indeed 本当に、実に 정말	
9. 电视	(名)	diànshì	television テレビ 텔레비죤	
10. 节目	(名)	jiémù	program 番組 프로그램	
11. 周末	(名)	zhōumò	weekend 週末 주말	
12. 爬	(动)	pá	to climb 登る 올라가다	
13. 山	(名)	shān	mountain 山 산	
14. 西	(名)	xī	west 西 서	
15. 座	(量)	zuò	(measure word for) mountain, building, etc. 比較的大型のものを数える 산이나 건축물등의 비교적 큰 물체를 세는 단위	
16. 漂亮	(形)	piàoliang	pretty, beautiful きれい．美しい 예쁘다	
17. 累	(形)	lèi	tired 疲れる 피곤하다	
18. 逛	(动)	guàng	to stroll, to ramble, to roam ぶらぶら歩く、ぶらつく 한가롭게 거닐다	
19. 街	(名)	jiē	street 街 길	
20. 更	(副)	gèng	more さらに、もっと 더욱	
21. 体育	(名)	tǐyù	physical training, sports スポーツ、体育 체육	

22. 运动	（名、动）	yùndòng	sports; movement, physical exercise 運動・運動する 운동
23. 打(球)	（动）	dǎ(qiú)	to play 球技をする 치다
24. 乒乓球	（名）	pīngpāngqiú	table tennis 卓球 탁구
25. 队	（名）	duì	team チーム、隊 팀
26. 差不多	（副）	chàbuduō	almost, about ほとんど 거의 비슷하다
27. 难	（形）	nán	difficult 難しい 어렵다
28. 学	（动）	xué	to study, to learn 学ぶ、習 배우다
29. 因为	（连）	yīnwèi	because 〜なので 왜냐하면

◆ 专名　Proper nouns

中文	（名）	Zhōngwén	Chinese 中国語 중문

◆ 补充词语　Additional words

1. 爱	（动）	ài	to like, to love 好き 좋아하다
2. 记	（动）	jì	to remember 覚える 기억하다
3. 容易	（形）	róngyì	easy 簡単、やさしい 쉽다
4. 商店	（名）	shāngdiàn	shop 商店、店 가게
5. 自己	（代）	zìjǐ	oneself 自分で 자기

6.	出租车	（名）	chūzūchē	TAXI タクシー 택시
7.	公共汽车		gōnggòng qìchē	bus バス 버스
8.	词语	（名）	cíyǔ	word and phrase 語句 단어와 어구
9.	附近	（名）	fùjìn	vicinity 付近 근처

第二十一课　八点我正在教室上课呢

◆ 生词　New words

1.	正	（副）	zhèng	to indicate an action in progress ちょうど〜している 바로, 지금
2.	接	（动）	jiē	to pick up (the phone) （電話に）出る 받다
3.	哎呀	（叹）	āiyā	Oh, my! 惊きを表すときに発する「おや」 이런, 아이고
4.	电	（名）	diàn	electricity 電気 전기
5.	忘	（动）	wàng	to forget 忘れる 잊다, 망각하다
6.	充电		chōng diàn	to charge 充電する 충전하다
7.	书法	（名）	shūfǎ	calligraphy 書道 서도
8.	张	（量）	zhāng	(measure word for) papers 紙や皮など平らなものを数える．枚． 장
9.	电影	（名）	diànyǐng	movie, film 映画 영화
10.	票	（名）	piào	ticket 切符．チケット 표

11. 约	（动）	yuē	to make (an appointment) 誘う．招く． 약속하다
12. 进步	（动、形）	jìnbù	to make a progress; progressive 進歩する 진보하다, 진보적인
13. 哪里	（代）	nǎli	a polite response to a compliment どこ；どういたしまして 무슨 말씀을
14. 课本	（名）	kèběn	textbook 教科書 교과서
15. 认识	（动）	rènshi	to know, to recognize 知っている、見たことがある 알아보다
16. 会	（助动、动）	huì	can; be able to 〜することができる 할 수 있다
17. 写	（动）	xiě	to write 書く 쓰다
18. 办	（动）	bàn	to do, to manage する、やる 처리하다
19. 办法	（名）	bànfǎ	method 方法 방법
20. 跟	（介、连、动）	gēn	with; and; follow 〜と（いっしょに） 하고
21. 怕	（副、动）	pà	be afraid of; fear 心配する、気にかかる 두렵다
22. 只要……就……		zhǐyào……jiù……	so long as 〜さえすれば〜 만 한다면…하다
23. 字	（名）	zì	character 字 글자
24. 记住		jìzhù	remember しっかり覚える 기억하다
25. 读	（动）	dú	to read 読む 읽다
26. 课文	（名）	kèwén	text 教科書中の本文 본문

27. 拼音	（名）	pīnyīn	alphabetic system ピンイン（表音式表記） 병음
28. 最	（副）	zuì	the most 最も 제일
29. 不要	（副）	búyào	don't 〜してはいけない 하지 말라

◆ **专名** Proper nouns

刘伟		Liú Wěi	(a name of a Chinese) 劉偉（人名） 유위

◆ **补充词语** Additional words

1. 去年	（名）	qùnián	last year 去年 작년
2. 火车	（名）	huǒchē	train 汽車、電車 기차
3. 大学	（名）	dàxué	university 大学 대학

第二十二课　旅行回来了

◆ **生词** New words

1. 回来		huílái	to return, to come back 帰って来る．戻って来る． 되돌아오다
2. 打算	（动、名）	dǎsuan	to intend; plan 〜するつもりである、〜する予定である 하려고 한다
3. 过	（动）	guò	to spend (time) 過ごす、たつ 보내다
4. 离	（动）	lí	to leave, indicate an interval of space, time, ect. 離れる・〜から、〜まで 로 부터
5. 俩	（数）	liǎ	two 二人、二つ 둘

6. 安排	（动、名）	ānpái	to arrange; arrangement 計画を立てる、手配する 배정하다
7. 好玩儿	（形）	hǎowánr	to have great fun, funny おもしろい 재미 있다
8. 晚饭	（名）	wǎnfàn	dinner, supper 夕食 저녁밥
9. 洗澡		xǐ zǎo	to take a shower (bath) 風呂に入る 샤워하다, 목욕하다
10. 得	（助动）	děi	must, have to 〜ねばならない．〜する必要がある 〜해야 한다
11. 公里	（量）	gōnglǐ	kilometre キロメートル 킬로미터
12. 骑	（动）	qí	to ride 乗る（馬、自転車、オートバイなど） 타다
13. 路上	（名）	lùshang	on the way 道中、途中 길에서
14. 一边……一边……		yībiān……yībiān……	do sth while doing sth else at the same time 〜しながら〜する 한편으로 …그리고 또 한편으로는
15. 唱	（动）	chàng	to sing 歌う (노래를) 부르다
16. 歌	（名）	gē	song 歌 노래
17. 出来		chūlai	come out 出てくる 나오다
18. 顿	（量）	dùn	(measure word for meals, etc.) 動作の回数を表す（食事、忠告など） 〜끼(밥을 세는 단위)
19. 刚	（副）	gāng	just now 〜したばかりである 금방
20. 一块儿	（副）	yíkuàir	together いっしょに 함께
21. 汤	（名）	tāng	soup スープ 국, 탕

22. 以为	（动）	yǐwéi	to think, to believe
			〜と思う
			여기다
23. 中餐	（名）	zhōngcān	Chinese food
			中華料理
			중국 음식
24. 笑	（动）	xiào	to smile, to laugh
			笑う
			웃다
25. 介绍	（动）	jièshào	to introduce
			紹介する
			소개하다
26. 凉	（形）	liáng	cool
			冷たい
			찬, 차가운
27. 饮料	（名）	yǐnliào	beverage
			飲料
			음료
28. 最后	（名）	zuìhòu	final, last
			最後
			마지막
29. 有时候		yǒu shíhou	sometimes
			時には
			어떨 때는
30. 水果	（名）	shuǐguǒ	fruit
			フルーツ、果物
			과일

◆ 补充词语　Additional words

1. 句	（量）	jù	(measure word for) words
			言葉を数える量詞
			구
2. 乌龙茶	（名）	wūlóngchá	oolong tea
			ウーロン茶
			우롱차
3. 着	（动）	zháo	used after a verb to indicate accomplishment or a result
			動作の結果を表す
			졌다(목적이 달성했음을 뜻함)
4. 打工		dǎ gōng	to do manual work
			アルバイトをする
			임시로 일하다
5. 重要	（形）	zhòngyào	important
			重要である、大切である
			중요하다
6. 厚	（形）	hòu	thick
			厚い
			두껍다

7.	成绩	（名）	chéngjì	result, mark, score 成績, 結果 성적
8.	经历	（名）	jīnglì	experience 経験 경험

第二十三课　穿什么衣服合适？

◆ 生 词　New words

1.	穿	（动）	chuān	to wear, to put on 着る 입다
2.	衣服	（名）	yīfu	clothing 服 옷
3.	合适	（形）	héshì	suitable ちょうどよい 어울린다
4.	外边	（名）	wàibian	outside 外側．外 바깥, 밖
5.	天气预报		tiānqì yùbào	weather forecast 天気予報 일기예보
6.	太阳	（名）	tàiyang	sun 太陽 태양
7.	大衣	（名）	dàyī	coat オーバー（コート） 외투
8.	暖和	（形）	nuǎnhuo	warm 暖かい 따뜻하다
9.	厚	（形）	hòu	thick 厚い 두껍다
10.	羽绒服	（名）	yǔróngfú	down-filled coat ダウンジャケット 오리털 옷
11.	麻烦	（动、名、形）	máfan	to bother; trouble; inconvenient 面倒をかける．煩わしい．迷惑 귀찮게 하다, 말썽, 성가시다
12.	样子	（名）	yàngzi	appearance 形、格好 모양

13.	好看	（形）	hǎokàn	good-looking きれい、美しい 보기 좋다
14.	试	（动）	shì	to try 試す 해보다
15.	镜子	（名）	jìngzi	mirror 鏡 거울
16.	瘦	（形）	shòu	slim, thin 小さくて窮屈である 꼭 낀다
17.	短	（形）	duǎn	short 短い 짧다
18.	个子	（名）	gèzi	height 背丈、身長 키
19.	高	（形）	gāo	tall 高い 크다
20.	大号	（形）	dàhào	large size 大きいサイズ,Lサイズ 크기
21.	肥	（形）	féi	fat, wide (of clothing, shoes ect.) ゆったりしている 풍성하다
22.	算了	（形）	suànle	forget it, never mind, let it be やめにする 그만두다
23.	长	（动）	zhǎng	to grow 生える,成長する 자라다
24.	别的	（代）	biéde	other 別のもの 다른
25.	带	（动）	dài	to bring, to carry with 持つ 가져오다
26.	商店	（名）	shāngdiàn	shop, store 商店 가게

◆ 补充词语　Additional words

1.	胖	（形）	pàng	fat 太っている 뚱뚱하다

2. 遍　　　　（量）　　　biàn　　　　(measure word)
　　　　　　　　　　　　　　　　　回、へん（動作の回数を数える）
　　　　　　　　　　　　　　　　　번, 차례

3. 零钱　　　（名）　　　língqián　　small change
　　　　　　　　　　　　　　　　　小銭
　　　　　　　　　　　　　　　　　잔돈

4. 毛笔　　　（名）　　　máobǐ　　　brush pen
　　　　　　　　　　　　　　　　　筆
　　　　　　　　　　　　　　　　　붓

第二十四课　你家有什么人？

◆ 生词 New words

1. 明年　　　（名）　　　míngnián　　next year
　　　　　　　　　　　　　　　　　来年
　　　　　　　　　　　　　　　　　내년

2. 大学　　　（名）　　　dàxué　　　university
　　　　　　　　　　　　　　　　　大学
　　　　　　　　　　　　　　　　　대학

3. 毕业　　　　　　　　　bì yè　　　graduate
　　　　　　　　　　　　　　　　　卒業
　　　　　　　　　　　　　　　　　졸업하다

4. 留学　　　　　　　　　liú xué　　to study abroad
　　　　　　　　　　　　　　　　　留学
　　　　　　　　　　　　　　　　　유학하다

5. 爸爸　　　（名）　　　bàba　　　　father
　　　　　　　　　　　　　　　　　おとうさん
　　　　　　　　　　　　　　　　　아빠

6. 工作　　　（名、动）　gōngzuò　　job; to work
　　　　　　　　　　　　　　　　　仕事、仕事をする
　　　　　　　　　　　　　　　　　일

7. 律师　　　（名）　　　lǜshī　　　lawyer
　　　　　　　　　　　　　　　　　弁護士
　　　　　　　　　　　　　　　　　변호사

8. 医生　　　（名）　　　yīshēng　　doctor
　　　　　　　　　　　　　　　　　医者
　　　　　　　　　　　　　　　　　의사

9. 哥哥　　　（名）　　　gēge　　　　elder brother
　　　　　　　　　　　　　　　　　兄
　　　　　　　　　　　　　　　　　오빠, 형

10. 妹妹　　　（名）　　　mèimei　　　younger sister
　　　　　　　　　　　　　　　　　妹
　　　　　　　　　　　　　　　　　여동생

11. 里　　　　（名）　　　lǐ　　　　　in, inside
　　　　　　　　　　　　　　　　　中
　　　　　　　　　　　　　　　　　안 쪽

12. 上(学)	(动)	shàng (xué)	to go to (school) 通う；通学する 공부하다
13. 中学	(名)	zhōngxué	middle school, high school 中学、高校 중학
14. 会	(助动)	huì	to be able to 〜のはずだ、〜するであろう 할 수 있다
15. 热情	(形)	rèqíng	warmhearted 心がこもっている．親切である． 열정적이다
16. 研究生	(名)	yánjiūshēng	postgraduate 大学院生 (석사, 박사) 연구생
17. 口	(量)	kǒu	(measure word) for family member, etc. 人数、人口を数える 식구
18. 大学生	(名)	dàxuéshēng	college student 大学生 대학생
19. 中学生	(名)	zhōngxuéshēng	middle school student 中学生、高校生 중학생
20. 照片	(名)	zhàopiàn	photo 写真 사진
21. 全	(形)	quán	all, whole そろっている 전체의
22. 女孩儿	(名)	nǚháir	young girl 女の子 여자 아이
23. 后边	(名)	hòubian	behind 後、後ろのほう 뒤 쪽
24. 红	(形)	hóng	red 赤い 빨간
25. 错	(形)	cuò	wrong, incorrect まちがっている 틀리다
26. 前边	(名)	qiánbian	in front of 前、前方 앞 쪽
27. 像	(动)	xiàng	to resemble 似ている 비슷하다

◆ 补充词语　Additional words

1.	弟弟	（名）	dìdi	younger brother 弟 남동생
2.	儿子	（名）	érzi	son 息子 아들
3.	幼儿园	（名）	yòu'éryuán	kindergarten 幼稚園 유치원
4.	女儿	（名）	nǚ'ér	daughter 娘 딸
5.	高中	（名）	gāozhōng	high school 高校 고등학교
6.	世界	（名）	shìjiè	world 世界 세계
7.	眼睛	（名）	yǎnjing	eye 目 눈
8.	老虎	（名）	lǎohǔ	tiger トラ 호랑이
9.	猫	（名）	māo	cat 猫 고양이
10.	年级	（名）	niánjí	grade 学年 학년

第二十五课　寒假打算怎么过？

◆ 生词　New words

1.	结束	（动）	jiéshù	to finish, to end 終わる 끝나다, 마치다
2.	一……就……		yī……jiù……	once..., as soon as... ひとたび〜すればすぐ〜 하자말자…곧
3.	回国		huí guó	to go back to one's own country 帰国する 귀국하다

4. 申请	（动、名）	shēnqǐng	to apply；application 申し込み．申し込む 신청하다, 신청
5. 延长	（动）	yáncháng	to extend 延長する 연장하다
6. 老家	（名）	lǎojiā	hometown 故郷、田舎 고향
7. 们	（尾）	men	(to form a plural) たち、等（クラスメートたち） (학우)들
8. 开(会)	（动）	kāi (huì)	to have (a meeting) 開く (회의를) 열다
9. 晚会	（名）	wǎnhuì	evening party パーティー 파티
10. 庆祝	（动）	qìngzhù	to celebrate 慶祝する．祝う． 경축하다
11. 新年	（名）	xīnnián	New Year 新年 새해
12. 需要	（动）	xūyào	to need 要る 필요하다
13. ……的话	（助）	……dehuà	if もし ~한다면
14. 或者	（连）	huòzhě	or あるいは ~이던가 아니면~이다
15. 决定	（动）	juédìng	to decide 決定する 결정하다
16. 飞机	（名）	fēijī	airplane 飛行機 비행기
17. 火车	（名）	huǒchē	train 汽車 기차
18. 预订	（动）	yùdìng	to book in advance 予約する 예약하다
19. 可能	（副）	kěnéng	perhaps, probably かもしれない 아마도, 아마

20. 这些	（代）	zhèxiē	these これら 이런 것들, 이러한
21. 查	（动）	chá	to check 調べる 검사하다, 조사하다
22. 南方	（名）	nánfāng	south 南の方 남쪽, 남방 지역
23. 左右	（名）	zuǒyòu	left and right, about 左と右 주위, 옆
24. 然后	（连）	ránhòu	then, afterwards そして 그런 후에
25. 大家	（代）	dàjiā	everyone みなさん 모두, 다들
26. 假期	（名）	jiàqī	holiday, vacation 休暇 휴가(휴일, 방학)기간
27. 愉快	（形）	yúkuài	happy, joyful, pleasant 嬉しい 기쁘다, 유쾌하다

◆ 专名 Proper nouns

1. 春节		Chūn Jié	Spring Festival 旧暦のお正月 춘절(구정)
2. 元旦		Yuándàn	New Year's Day 元日 설날, 정월 초하루
3. 昆明		Kūnmíng	Kunming 昆明 쿤밍, 곤명
4. 云南		Yúnnán	Yunnan 云南 윈난성, 운남성
5. 海南		Hǎinán	Hainan 海南 하이난성, 해남성

◆ 补充词语 Additional words

1. 紧张	（形）	jǐnzhāng	nervous 緊張する 긴장하다

2. 健康　　　（形）　　　jiànkāng　　　healthy
健康である
건강하다
3. 大海　　　（名）　　　dàhǎi　　　sea
海
바다, 대해

词语总表

词语 Words	词性 Part of speech	拼音 Phonetic Transcription	所在课 Lesson
A			
阿姨	(名)	āyí	14
啊	(助)	a	12
哎呀	(叹)	āiyā	21
爱好	(名)	àihào	18
安排	(动、名)	ānpái	22
B			
八	(数)	bā	6
吧	(助)	ba	9
爸爸	(名)	bàba	24
百	(数)	bǎi	8
班	(名、量)	bān	5
办	(动)	bàn	21
办法	(名)	bànfǎ	21
办公室	(名)	bàngōngshì	9
半	(数)	bàn	6
帮	(动)	bāng	13
饱	(形)	bǎo	17
本	(量)	běn	13
比	(介)	bǐ	17
毕业		bì yè	24
边	(名)	biān	7
别	(副)	bié	17
别的	(代)	biéde	23
别人	(代)	biérén	16
病	(动、名)	bìng	10
不	(副)	bù	5
不错	(形)	búcuò	14
不过	(连)	búguò	13
不客气		bú kèqi	16
不太	(副)	bútài	12
不要	(副)	búyào	21
不用	(副)	búyòng	7
C			
才	(副)	cái	10

58

菜	(名)	cài	8
菜单	(名)	càidān	17
参加	(动)	cānjiā	18
厕所	(名)	cèsuǒ	7
层	(量)	céng	16
茶	(名)	chá	11
查	(动)	chá	25
差	(动)	chà	6
差不多	(副)	chàbuduō	20
长	(形)	cháng	15
尝	(动)	cháng	11
唱	(动)	chàng	22
车	(名)	chē	8
吃	(动)	chī	11
充电		chōng diàn	21
出来		chūlái	22
出去		chūqù	19
穿	(动)	chuān	23
春天	(名)	chūntiān	14
次	(量)	cì	18
从	(介)	cóng	18
从……到……		cóng……dào……	6
错	(形)	cuò	24

D

……的话	(助)	……dehuà	25
答应	(动)	dāying	18
打(电话)	(动)	dǎ(diànhuà)	9
打(球)	(动)	dǎ(qiú)	20
打包		dǎ bāo	17
打算	(动、名)	dǎsuan	22
大	(形)	dà	7
大概	(副、形)	dàgài	11
大号	(形)	dàhào	23
大家	(代)	dàjiā	25
大使馆	(名)	dàshǐguǎn	10
大学	(名)	dàxué	24
大学生	(名)	dàxuéshēng	24
大衣	(名)	dàyī	23
大夫	(名)	dàifu	16
带	(动)	dài	23
担心		dān xīn	17
单	(名)	dān	13

59

当然	（形）	dāngrán	12
到	（动）	dào	16
得	（动）	dé	19
地	（助）	de	18
的	（助）	de	4
得	（助）	de	18
得	（助动）	děi	22
等	（动）	děng	19
地方	（名）	dìfang	7
第	（头）	dì	15
点	（量、名）	diǎn	6
点（菜）	（动）	diǎn (cài)	17
点心	（名）	diǎnxin	11
电	（名）	diàn	21
电话	（名）	diànhuà	9
电视	（名）	diànshì	20
电影	（名）	diànyǐng	21
订单	（名）	dìngdān	13
冬天	（名）	dōngtiān	14
懂	（动）	dǒng	9
动物园	（名）	dòngwùyuán	16
都	（副）	dōu	4
读	（动）	dú	21
短	（形）	duǎn	23
队	（名）	duì	20
对	（形）	duì	5
对不起	（动）	duìbuqǐ	10
对方	（名）	duìfāng	13
顿	（量）	dùn	22
多	（代）	duō	15
多	（形）	duō	15
多大		duō dà	5
多少	（代）	duōshao	8

E

饿	（形）	è	17
二	（数）	èr	5
二十	（数）	èrshí	5

F

发烧		fā shāo	19
饭	（名）	fàn	14
饭馆儿	（名）	fànguǎnr	17
方便	（形）	fāngbiàn	13

房间	（名）	fángjiān	10
放（假）	（动）	fàng (jià)	15
放心		fàng xīn	14
飞机	（名）	fēijī	25
非常	（副）	fēicháng	14
肥	（形）	féi	23
分	（量、名）	fēn	6
分钟	（量）	fēnzhōng	16
风	（名）	fēng	14
服务员	（名）	fúwùyuán	8
辅导	（动）	fǔdǎo	18
付款		fù kuǎn	13
复习	（动）	fùxí	20

G

该……了		gāi……le	6
改天	（副）	gǎitiān	19
干	（动）	gàn	12
感冒	（动、名）	gǎnmào	10
刚	（副）	gāng	22
刚才	（名）	gāngcái	13
高	（形）	gāo	23
高兴	（形）	gāoxìng	12
告诉	（动）	gàosu	10
哥哥	（名）	gēge	24
歌	（名）	gē	22
个	（量）	gè	9
个子	（名）	gèzi	23
给	（介、动）	gěi	9
跟	（介、连、动）	gēn	21
更	（副）	gèng	20
工作	（名、动）	gōngzuò	24
公里	（量）	gōnglǐ	22
够	（动、副）	gòu	17
拐	（动）	guǎi	16
关	（动）	guān	13
关心	（动）	guānxīn	19
光临	（动）	guānglín	17
逛	（动）	guàng	20
国	（名）	guó	5
过	（动）	guò	22
过	（助）	guo	15

H

还	（副）	hái	8
还可以		hái kěyǐ	14
还是	（连、副）	háishi	11
寒假	（名）	hánjià	15
汉字	（名）	Hànzì	15
好	（形）	hǎo	4
好吃	（形）	hǎochī	11
好好儿	（副）	hǎohāor	19
好看	（形）	hǎokàn	23
好玩儿	（形）	hǎowánr	22
好像	（副）	hǎoxiàng	12
号	（量、名）	hào	9
号码	（名）	hàomǎ	9
喝	（动）	hē	11
合适	（形）	héshì	23
和	（连、介）	hé	13
黑	（形）	hēi	8
很	（副）	hěn	7
红	（形）	hóng	24
后边	（名）	hòubian	24
厚	（形）	hòu	23
互相	（副）	hùxiāng	18
花	（动）	huā	8
欢迎	（动）	huānyíng	11
回	（动）	huí	10
回答	（动）	huídá	12
回国		huí guó	25
回来		huílái	22
回去		huíqù	19
会	（助动、动）	huì	21
会	（助动）	huì	24
火车	（名）	huǒchē	25
或者	（连）	huòzhě	25

J

……极了		……jíle	19
几	（代）	jǐ	5
记住		jìzhù	21
季节	（名）	jìjié	14
寄	（动）	jì	13
家	（名）	jiā	12
价钱	（名）	jiàqián	13
假期	（名）	jiàqī	25

见	(动)	jiàn	18
件	(量)	jiàn	9
讲价		jiǎng jià	11
饺子	(名)	jiǎozi	11
叫	(动)	jiào	4
教	(动)	jiāo	18
教室	(名)	jiàoshì	7
接	(动)	jiē	21
街	(名)	jiē	20
节	(量、名)	jié	15
节目	(名)	jiémù	20
结束	(动)	jiéshù	25
结账		jié zhàng	17
介绍	(动)	jièshào	22
借	(动)	jiè	13
斤	(量)	jīn	11
今年	(名)	jīnnián	5
今天	(名)	jīntiān	6
进	(动)	jìn	10
进步	(动、形)	jìnbù	21
进来		jìnlái	12
镜子	(名)	jìngzi	23
九	(数)	jiǔ	6
旧	(形)	jiù	20
决定	(动)	juédìng	25
觉得	(动)	juéde	12

K

咖啡	(名)	kāfēi	11
开	(动)	kāi	12
开(会)	(动)	kāi (huì)	25
开始	(动)	kāishǐ	18
开玩笑		kāi wánxiào	19
开学		kāi xué	15
看	(动)	kàn	8
考	(动)	kǎo	19
考试	(动)	kǎoshì	15
咳嗽	(动)	késou	19
可能	(副)	kěnéng	25
可是	(连)	kěshì	12
可以	(助动)	kěyǐ	11
刻	(量)	kè	10
课	(名)	kè	6
课本	(名)	kèběn	21

课文	(名)	kèwén	21
口	(量)	kǒu	24
口语	(名)	kǒuyǔ	6
块(元)	(量)	kuài（yuán）	8
快	(形)	kuài	13
快递	(名)	kuàidì	13
快乐	(形)	kuàilè	9

L

啦	(助)	la	20
辣	(形)	là	17
来	(动)	lái	10
蓝	(形)	lán	8
蓝色	(名)	lánsè	8
老家	(名)	lǎojiā	25
老师	(名)	lǎoshī	4
累	(形)	lèi	20
冷	(形)	lěng	14
离	(动)	lí	22
礼物	(名)	lǐwù	9
里	(名)	lǐ	24
里面	(名)	lǐmian	17
厉害	(形)	lìhai	19
俩	(数)	liǎ	22
练习	(动、名)	liànxí	18
凉	(形)	liáng	22
两	(数)	liǎng	6
辆	(量)	liàng	8
聊	(动)	liáo	18
聊天儿		liáo tiānr	12
了	(助)	le	8
零(〇)	(数)	líng	9
留学		liú xué	24
留学生	(名)	liúxuéshēng	4
六	(数)	liù	9
楼	(名、量)	lóu	16
楼	(名)	lóu	9
录音		lù yīn	20
路人	(名)	lùrén	16
路上	(名)	lùshang	22
旅行	(动)	lǚxíng	18
律师	(名)	lǜshī	24

M

妈妈	（名）	māma	14
麻烦	（动、名、形）	máfan	23
马路	（名）	mǎlù	16
马上	（副）	mǎshàng	17
吗	（助）	ma	5
买	（动）	mǎi	8
卖	（动）	mài	16
馒头	（名）	mántou	11
慢	（形）	màn	19
忙	（形）	máng	14
毛（角）	（量）	máo (jiǎo)	8
没	（动、副）	méi	11
没关系		méi guānxi	19
没有	（动、副）	méiyǒu	6
每	（代）	měi	15
妹妹	（名）	mèimei	24
门	（名）	mén	12
门	（量）	mén	15
们	（尾）	men	25
米饭	（名）	mǐfàn	17
名字	（名）	míngzi	4
明年	（名）	míngnián	24
明天	（名）	míngtiān	6

N

哪	（代）	nǎ	5
哪儿	（代）	nǎr	7
哪个		nǎ ge	8
哪里	（代）	nǎli	21
那	（连）	nà	19
那	（代）	nà (nèi)	7
那边	（代）	nàbiān	8
那儿	（代）	nàr	7
那个		nà ge	7
男	（形）	nán	19
南方	（名）	nánfāng	25
难	（形）	nán	20
闹钟	（名）	nàozhōng	10
呢	（助）	ne	4
能	（助动）	néng	10
你	（代）	nǐ	4
你们	（代）	nǐmen	4

年	（名）	nián	15
您	（代）	nín	4
努力	（动、形）	nǔlì	19
女孩儿	（名）	nǚháir	24
暖和	（形）	nuǎnhuo	23

P

爬	（动）	pá	20
怕	（副、动）	pà	21
旁边	（名）	pángbiān	7
陪	（动）	péi	19
朋友	（名）	péngyou	12
啤酒	（名）	píjiǔ	17
便宜	（形）	piányi	11
票	（名）	piào	21
漂亮	（形）	piàoliang	20
拼音	（名）	pīnyīn	21
乒乓球	（名）	pīngpāngqiú	20
瓶	（量、名）	píng	17
葡萄	（名）	pútao	11

Q

七	（数）	qī	6
期末	（名）	qīmò	15
骑	（动）	qí	22
起床		qǐ chuáng	10
前	（名）	qián	16
前边	（名）	qiánbian	24
钱	（名）	qián	8
茄子	（名）	qiézi	17
清楚	（形）	qīngchu	16
请	（动）	qǐng	10
请假		qǐng jià	10
请问	（动）	qǐngwèn	7
庆祝	（动）	qìngzhù	25
秋天	（名）	qiūtiān	14
去	（动）	qù	10
全	（形）	quán	24

R

然后	（连）	ránhòu	25
让	（动）	ràng	14
热	（形）	rè	14
热情	（形）	rèqíng	24

人	(名)	rén	4
认识	(动)	rènshi	21
肉	(名)	ròu	17

S

三	(数)	sān	7
散步		sàn bù	19
山	(名)	shān	20
商店	(名)	shāngdiàn	23
上	(名)	shàng	19
上边	(名)	shàngbian	11
上课		shàng kè	6
上(楼)	(动)	shàng (lóu)	16
上(网)	(动)	shàng (wǎng)	13
上午	(名)	shàngwǔ	6
上(学)	(动)	shàng (xué)	24
少	(形)	shǎo	15
申请	(动、名)	shēnqǐng	25
身体	(名)	shēntǐ	14
什么	(代)	shénme	4
生词	(名)	shēngcí	12
生日	(名)	shēngrì	9
声调	(名)	shēngdiào	18
十九	(数)	shíjiǔ	5
时候	(名)	shíhou	15
时间	(名)	shíjiān	9
食堂	(名)	shítáng	7
事	(名)	shì	9
试	(动)	shì	23
是	(动)	shì	4
收	(动)	shōu	13
手机	(名)	shǒujī	18
售货员	(名)	shòuhuòyuán	8
瘦	(形)	shòu	23
书	(名)	shū	13
书法	(名)	shūfǎ	21
舒服	(形)	shūfu	19
暑假	(名)	shǔjià	15
谁	(代)	shuí (shéi)	5
水	(名)	shuǐ	19
水果	(名)	shuǐguǒ	22
水平	(名)	shuǐpíng	18
睡觉		shuì jiào	10
说	(动)	shuō	9

四	（数）	sì	8
送	（动）	sòng	19
送	（动）	sòng	13
宿舍	（名）	sùshè	7
酸	（形）	suān	11
算了	（形）	suànle	23
随便	（形）	suíbiàn	11
岁	（量）	suì	5
所以	（连）	suǒyǐ	10

T

他	（代）	tā	4
他们	（代）	tāmen	5
她	（代）	tā	4
太	（副）	tài	15
太阳	（名）	tàiyang	23
汤	（名）	tāng	22
特别	（副、形）	tèbié	14
疼	（形）	téng	10
体育	（名）	tǐyù	20
天	（名）	tiān	10
天气	（名）	tiānqì	14
天气预报		tiānqì yùbào	23
甜	（形）	tián	11
填	（动）	tián	13
听	（动）	tīng	12
听力	（名）	tīnglì	15
听说	（动）	tīngshuō	14
听写	（动、名）	tīngxiě	12
停	（动）	tíng	10
挺	（副）	tǐng	18
同学	（名）	tóngxué	16
头	（名）	tóu	10
图书馆	（名）	túshūguǎn	13

W

外边	（名）	wàibian	23
完	（动）	wán	11
玩儿	（动）	wánr	9
晚	（形）	wǎn	10
晚饭	（名）	wǎnfàn	22
晚会	（名）	wǎnhuì	25
晚上	（名）	wǎnshang	9
碗	（量、名）	wǎn	17

网	（名）	wǎng	13
往	（介）	wǎng	16
忘	（动）	wàng	21
为什么		wèi shénme	12
位	（量）	wèi	17
味道	（名）	wèidào	17
喂	（叹）	wèi	9
问	（动）	wèn	9
问题	（名）	wèntí	9
我	（代）	wǒ	4
我们	（代）	wǒmen	4
五十	（数）	wǔshí	6

X

西	（名）	xī	20
希望	（动、名）	xīwàng	18
习惯	（动、名）	xíguàn	11
洗澡		xǐ zǎo	22
喜欢	（动）	xǐhuan	8
下	（名）	xià	18
下（订单）	（动）	xià (dìngdān)	13
下（雨）	（动）	xià (yǔ)	14
下课		xià kè	16
下午	（名）	xiàwǔ	15
夏天	（名）	xiàtiān	14
先	（副、名）	xiān	19
先生	（名）	xiānsheng	16
现在	（名）	xiànzài	6
香	（形）	xiāng	17
想	（动）	xiǎng	12
想	（助动、动）	xiǎng	10
像	（动）	xiàng	24
小	（形）	xiǎo	14
小时	（名）	xiǎoshí	18
笑	（动）	xiào	22
鞋	（名）	xié	16
写	（动）	xiě	21
谢谢	（动）	xièxie	7
新	（形）	xīn	20
新年	（名）	xīnnián	25
星期	（名）	xīngqī	6
星期天	（名）	xīngqītiān	12
行	（动、形）	xíng	18
姓	（名、动）	xìng	4

休息	(动)	xiūxi	10
需要	(动)	xūyào	25
学	(动)	xué	20
学年	(名)	xuénián	15
学期	(名)	xuéqī	15
学生	(名)	xuésheng	7
学习	(动)	xuéxí	14
学校	(名)	xuéxiào	7

Y

牙	(名)	yá	16
(牙)科	(名)	(yá) kē	16
延长	(动)	yáncháng	25
研究生	(名)	yánjiūshēng	24
颜色	(名)	yánsè	8
样子	(名)	yàngzi	23
要	(助动、动)	yào	8
要是	(连)	yàoshi	13
也	(副)	yě	5
夜里	(名)	yèli	14
一	(数)	yī	5
一……就……		yī……jiù……	25
一般	(形)	yìbān	20
一边……一边……		yìbiān……yìbiān……	22
一点儿	(数量)	yìdiǎnr	11
一定	(副、形)	yídìng	18
一共	(副)	yígòng	8
一会儿	(数量)	yíhuìr	12
一块儿	(副)	yíkuàir	22
一起	(副)	yìqǐ	9
一下	(数量)	yíxià	13
一月	(名)	yīyuè	15
衣服	(名)	yīfu	23
医生	(名)	yīshēng	24
医院	(名)	yīyuàn	16
已经	(副)	yǐjīng	14
以后	(名)	yǐhòu	11
以前	(名)	yǐqián	11
以为	(动)	yǐwéi	22
因为	(连)	yīnwèi	20
音乐	(名)	yīnyuè	12
饮料	(名)	yǐnliào	22
有	(动)	yǒu	6
有(一)点儿	(副)	yǒu (yì) diǎnr	12

有时候		yǒu shíhou	22
有意思		yǒu yìsi	18
又……又……		yòu……yòu……	17
右	(名)	yòu	16
右边	(名)	yòubian	7
鱼	(名)	yú	17
愉快	(形)	yúkuài	25
羽绒服	(名)	yǔróngfú	23
雨	(名)	yǔ	14
语法	(名)	yǔfǎ	15
预订	(动)	yùdìng	25
预习	(动)	yùxí	20
远	(形)	yuǎn	16
约	(动)	yuē	21
月	(名)	yuè	15
运动	(名、动)	yùndòng	20

Z

再	(副)	zài	16
再见	(动)	zàijiàn	6
在	(动、介)	zài	5
咱们	(代)	zánmen	12
早	(形)	zǎo	5
早上	(名)	zǎoshang	5
怎么	(代)	zěnme	10
怎么样	(代)	zěnmeyàng	8
张	(量)	zhāng	21
长	(动)	zhǎng	23
着急		zháo jí	13
找	(动)	zhǎo	18
找(钱)	(动)	zhǎo(qián)	13
照片	(名)	zhàopiàn	24
这	(代)	zhè (zhèi)	7
这儿	(代)	zhèr	7
这个		zhè ge	7
这么	(代)	zhème	19
这些	(代)	zhèxiē	25
这样	(代)	zhèyàng	18
着	(助)	zhe	12
真	(形)	zhēn	12
真	(副)	zhēn	20
正	(副)	zhèng	21
知道	(动)	zhīdào	9
只	(副)	zhǐ	15

只要……就……		zhǐyào……jiù……	21
中餐	（名）	zhōngcān	22
中学	（名）	zhōngxué	24
中学生	（名）	zhōngxuéshēng	24
种	（量）	zhǒng	8
重	（形）	zhòng	19
周	（名）	zhōu	15
周末	（名）	zhōumò	20
住	（动）	zhù	9
祝	（动）	zhù	9
专业	（名）	zhuānyè	18
准备	（动）	zhǔnbèi	19
桌子	（名）	zhuōzi	11
自习	（动）	zìxí	13
自行车	（名）	zìxíngchē	8
字	（名）	zì	21
走	（动）	zǒu	16
最	（副）	zuì	21
最后	（名）	zuìhòu	22
最近	（名）	zuìjìn	14
昨天	（名）	zuótiān	12
左边	（名）	zuǒbian	7
左右	（名）	zuǒyòu	25
作业	（名）	zuòyè	9
坐	（动）	zuò	11
座	（量）	zuò	20
做	（动）	zuò	12

量 词 表

名词 Nouns	拼音 Phonetic Transcription	对应的量词 Measure words	所在课 Lesson
1. 阿姨	āyí	位 wèi、个 gè	14
2. 爱好	àihào	个 gè、种 zhǒng	18
3. 安排	ānpái	个 gè、种 zhǒng、项 xiàng	22
4. 爸爸	bàba	个 gè、位 wèi	24
5. 班	bān	个 gè	5
6. 办法	bànfǎ	个 gè、种 zhǒng	21
7. 办公室	bàngōngshì	个 gè、间 jiān	9
8. 病	bìng	种 zhǒng、个 gè	10
9. 菜	cài	个 gè、种 zhǒng、盘 pán、道 dào	8
10. 菜单	càidān	个 gè、张 zhāng、份 fèn	17
11. 厕所	cèsuǒ	个 gè	7
12. 茶	chá	杯 bēi、碗 wǎn、壶 hú、口 kǒu、种 zhǒng	11
13. 车	chē	辆 liàng	8
14. 春天	chūntiān	个 gè	14
15. 醋	cù	瓶 píng、碗 wǎn、杯 bēi、点儿 diǎnr、滴 dī、些 xiē	17
16. 大使馆	dàshǐguǎn	个 gè	10
17. 大学	dàxué	所 suǒ、个 gè	24
18. 大学生	dàxuéshēng	个 gè、位 wèi、些 xiē、群 qún	24
19. 大衣	dàyī	件 jiàn	23
20. 大夫	dàifu	位 wèi、个 gè	16
21. 地方	dìfang	个 gè、些 xiē	7
22. 点心	diǎnxin	个 gè、块 kuài、种 zhǒng、些 xiē、盘 pán	11
23. 电	diàn	度 dù、点儿 diǎnr	21
24. 电话	diànhuà	个 gè、部 bù	9
25. 电视	diànshì	台 tái	20
26. 电影	diànyǐng	部 bù、场 chǎng	21
27. 订单	dìngdān	个 gè、份 fèn、张 zhāng	13
28. 冬天	dōngtiān	个 gè	14
29. 动物园	dòngwùyuán	个 gè、座 zuò	16
30. 队	duì	个 gè、支 zhī	20
31. 饭	fàn	碗 wǎn、顿 dùn	14
32. 饭馆儿	fànguǎnr	个 gè、家 jiā	17
33. 房间	fángjiān	个 gè、间 jiān	10
34. 飞机	fēijī	架 jià	25
35. 风	fēng	阵 zhèn、股 gǔ、丝 sī	14
36. 服务员	fúwùyuán	位 wèi、个 gè	8
37. 辅导	fǔdǎo	位 wèi、个 gè	18
38. 感冒	gǎnmào	种 zhǒng	10

73

39. 哥哥	gēge	个 gè	24
40. 歌	gē	支 zhī、首 shǒu	22
41. 工作	gōngzuò	种 zhǒng、项 xiàng、份 fèn、个 gè	24
42. 寒假	hánjià	个 gè	15
43. 汉字	Hànzì	个 gè、些 xiē	15
44. 号码	hàomǎ	个 gè、种 zhǒng	9
45. 火车	huǒchē	列 liè、节 jié、辆 liàng	25
46. 鸡蛋	jīdàn	个 gè、斤 jīn	17
47. 季节	jìjié	个 gè	14
48. 家	jiā	个 gè	12
49. 假期	jiàqī	个 gè	25
50. 饺子	jiǎozi	个 gè、两 liǎng、斤 jīn、盘 pán、碗 wǎn	11
51. 教室	jiàoshì	间 jiān、个 gè	7
52. 街	jiē	条 tiáo	20
53. 节目	jiémù	个 gè	20
54. 镜子	jìngzi	面 miàn	23
55. 咖啡	kāfēi	杯 bēi、种 zhǒng	11
56. 考试	kǎoshì	个 gè、种 zhǒng、次 cì	15
57. 课	kè	门 mén、节 jié、种 zhǒng	6
58. 课本	kèběn	本 běn、种 zhǒng	21
59. 课文	kèwén	篇 piān、段 duàn	21
60. 快递	kuàidì	个 gè、份 fèn	13
61. 老师	lǎoshī	位 wèi、个 gè	4
62. 礼物	lǐwù	件 wèi、个 gè	9
63. 练习	liànxí	个 gè、种 zhǒng	18
64. 留学生	liúxuéshēng	个 gè、位 wèi	4
65. 楼	lóu	座 zuò、层 céng	9
66. 路人	lùrén	位 wèi、个 gè	16
67. 律师	lǜshī	位 wèi、个 gè	24
68. 妈妈	māma	个 gè、位 wèi	14
69. 马路	mǎlù	条 tiáo	16
70. 馒头	mántou	个 gè、斤 jīn、块 kuài	11
71. 妹妹	mèimei	个 gè	24
72. 门	mén	个 gè	12
73. 米饭	mǐfàn	碗 wǎn、两 liǎng	17
74. 名字	míngzi	个 gè	4
75. 闹钟	nàozhōng	个 gè	10
76. 牛	niú	头 tóu	17
77. 女孩儿	nǚháir	个 gè	24
78. 朋友	péngyou	位 wèi、个 gè	12
79. 啤酒	píjiǔ	瓶 píng、杯 bēi	17
80. 票	piào	张 zhāng	21
81. 拼音	pīnyīn	个 gè	21
82. 乒乓球	pīngpāngqiú	个 gè	20

83. 葡萄	pútao	个 gè、串 chuàn、斤 jīn	11
84. 钱	qián	块 kuài、元 yuán、毛 máo、角 jiǎo、分 fēn、些 xiē	8
85. 茄子	qiézi	个 gè	17
86. 秋天	qiūtiān	个 gè	14
87. 人	rén	个 gè、口 kǒu、种 zhǒng、些 xiē	4
88. 肉	ròu	块 kuài、种 zhǒng、斤 jīn	17
89. 山	shān	座 zuò	20
90. 商店	shāngdiàn	个 gè、家 jiā	23
91. 上午	shàngwǔ	个 gè	6
92. 生词	shēngcí	个 gè、些 xiē	12
93. 生日	shēngrì	个 gè	9
94. 声调	shēngdiào	种 zhǒng	18
95. 时间	shíjiān	段 duàn、点儿 diǎnr、些 xiē	9
96. 食堂	shítáng	个 gè	7
97. 事	shì	件 jiàn	9
98. 手机	shǒujī	个 gè、种 zhǒng	18
99. 售货员	shòuhuòyuán	个 gè、位 wèi	8
100. 书	shū	本 běn	13
101. 暑假	shǔjià	个 gè	15
102. 水	shuǐ	杯 bēi、瓶 píng、碗 wǎn、公升 gōngshēng	19
103. 水果	shuǐguǒ	种 zhǒng	22
104. 水平	shuǐpíng	种 zhǒng	18
105. 宿舍	sùshè	间 jiān	7
106. 太阳	tàiyang	个 gè	23
107. 汤	tāng	碗 wǎn、种 zhǒng	22
108. 糖	táng	块 kuài、点儿 diǎnr、些 xiē、斤 jīn、种 zhǒng	17
109. 天气	tiānqì	种 zhǒng	14
110. 同学	tóngxué	位 wèi、个 gè	16
111. 头	tóu	个 gè	10
112. 图书馆	túshūguǎn	座 zuò、个 gè	13
113. 晚饭	wǎnfàn	顿 dùn	22
114. 晚会	wǎnhuì	个 gè	25
115. 晚上	wǎnshang	个 gè	9
116. 碗	wǎn	个 gè	17
117. 味道	wèidào	种 zhǒng	17
118. 问题	wèntí	个 gè、些 xiē	9
119. 希望	xīwàng	个 gè	18
120. 习惯	xíguàn	种 zhǒng、个 gè	11
121. 下午	xiàwǔ	个 gè	15
122. 夏天	xiàtiān	个 gè	14
123. 先生	xiānsheng	位 wèi、个 gè	16
124. 小时	xiǎoshí	个 gè	18
125. 鞋	xié	双 shuāng、只 zhī	16
126. 新年	xīnnián	个 gè	25

127.星期	xīngqī	个 gè	6
128.星期天	xīngqītiān	个 gè	12
129.姓	xìng	个 gè、种 zhǒng	4
130.学年	xuénián	个 gè	15
131.学期	xuéqī	个 gè	15
132.学生	xuésheng	个 gè、些 xiē	7
133.学校	xuéxiào	所 suǒ、座 zuò、个 gè	7
134.牙	yá	个 gè、颗 kē	16
135.研究生	yánjiūshēng	个 gè	24
136.颜色	yánsè	种 zhǒng	8
137.样子	yàngzi	种 zhǒng	23
138.衣服	yīfu	件 jiàn、套 tào	23
139.医生	yīshēng	位 wèi、个 gè	24
140.医院	yīyuàn	家 jiā、座 zuò	16
141.音乐	yīnyuè	种 zhǒng、段 duàn	12
142.饮料	yǐnliào	杯 bēi、瓶 píng、种 zhǒng	22
143.鱼	yú	条 tiáo、斤 jīn、种 zhǒng	17
144.羽绒服	yǔróngfú	件 jiàn	23
145.雨	yǔ	点儿 diǎnr、阵 zhèn、场 chǎng	14
146.语法	yǔfǎ	种 zhǒng、个 gè	15
147.月	yuè	个 gè	15
148.运动	yùndòng	种 zhǒng、项 xiàng	20
149.早上	zǎoshang	个 gè	5
150.照片	zhàopiàn	张 zhāng	24
151.中餐	zhōngcān	顿 dùn	22
152.中学	zhōngxué	所 suǒ、座 zuò	24
153.中学生	zhōngxuéshēng	个 gè	24
154.周末	zhōumò	个 gè	20
155.专业	zhuānyè	个 gè、种 zhǒng	18
156.桌子	zhuōzi	张 zhāng	11
157.字	zì	个 gè、些 xiē	21
158.自行车	zìxíngchē	辆 liàng	8
159.作业	zuòyè	个 gè、些 xiē	9

语言点索引

语言点	所在课	页码
你好！	4	20
你叫什么名字？	4	21
你呢？	4	21
早上好！早！	5	26
你多大？	5	26
你在几班？	5	26
百以内的数字	5	26
时间表示法	6	34
今天星期几？	6	34
上午从八点到九点五十分上口语课	6	34
"二"和"两"	6	34
你该上课了	6	35
请问	7	42
不用谢	7	42
简单方位词：旁边、左边、右边	7	42
指示代词：这、那、哪	7	43
人民币的单位和读法	8	49
黑的、蓝的都有	8	49
量词：个、辆、种	8	49
我买了一辆蓝的	8	49
看看/问问/玩儿玩儿	9	56
号码的读法	9	56
喂，是王平吗？	9	56
祝他生日快乐！	9	57
你怎么了？	10	64
安妮今天不能来上课了	10	64
你怎么才来？	10	65
请假	10	65
没问题	11	73
酸不酸？	11	74
"可以"和"能"	11	74
斤	11	74
茶还是咖啡？	11	74
我有点儿想家	12	82
"咱们"和"我们"	12	82
门开着/听着音乐聊聊天儿	12	83
做作业呢	12	83
真的吗？	12	83
要是你现在有时间，就和我一起去吧。	13	90

"不过"和"可是"	13	90
没有借到/送到我宿舍/寄到上海	13	91
今天上午书就送到我宿舍了	13	91
您填一下快递单。	13	91
天气怎么样？/身体怎么样？	14	99
程度的表示：不错 还可以	14	99
王阿姨	14	100
听说你病了	14	100
请告诉我妈妈	14	100
老师说过	15	106
寒假有多长时间？	15	106
"一月"和"一个月"	15	107
一共有十九周	15	107
称呼：先生/同学/大夫	16	116
马路左边就是	16	116
走几分钟就到了	16	116
太谢谢你了	16	116
我喜欢又酸又甜的/我觉得那儿的菜又好吃又便宜	17	125
有糖醋鱼、西红柿炒鸡蛋什么的	17	125
来个西红柿炒鸡蛋怎么样？	17	125
我也说不清楚/吃不完的菜打包吧	17	125
这儿的菜比食堂的菜香多了	17	126
那不行	18	134
这样吧	18	135
王平高兴地答应了	18	135
王平辅导得怎么样？	18	135
挺好的	18	135
"有点儿"和"一点儿"	19	143
你回去好好儿休息休息	19	143
没关系	19	143
"没"和"没有"	19	144
慢走	19	144
做作业啦、听录音啦、复习旧课啦、预习新课啦……	20	153
你真是个好学生	20	153
差不多	20	153
我觉得爬山太累	20	154
你是几点给我打的？	21	164
八点我正在教室上课呢。	21	164
哪里	21	164
只要多看多写，就一定能学好。	21	165
快到周末了/食堂快关门了/我都快吃完了	22	172
我想先洗个澡，再去吃饭。	22	172
路上一边骑，一边唱歌。	22	172
你不是正在喝汤吗？	22	173

你以为吃中餐是先喝汤啊！	22	173
还是不合适	23	181
算了	23	182
一天比一天冷了	23	182
没有一件合适的	23	182
上中学	24	189
那还用说	24	190
全家	24	190
你们俩长得太像了	24	190
我一放假就回国。	25	196
"元旦"和"春节"	25	196
不用准备什么。	25	197
我想去好几个地方呢。	25	197

Lesson Four   May I ask your name?

（一）

(The first day of classes, on campus)

Jeff:　　　Hello!
Annie:　　Hello!
Jeff:　　　My name is Jeff. What is you name?
Annie:　　My name is Annie.

（二）

(In the classroom)

Ms. Tian:　　　How do you do? *(I am the teacher of this class.)* My last name is Tian.
Anne & Jeff:　 How do you do Ms. Tian?
Ms. Tian:　　　*(To Jeff)* What is your name?
Jeff:　　　　　 My name is Jeff.
Ms. Tian:　　　*(To Annie)* And you?
Annie:　　　　 My name is Annie.

（三）

(Outside the classroom)

Wang Ping:　　Hello!
Jeff & Annie:　 Hello!
Jeff:　　　　　 What is your name?
Wang Ping:　　My name is Wang Ping. I am Chinese. You are...?
Annie:　　　　 We are both foreign students. My name is Annie. His name is Jeff.

（四）

(Jeff says to Wang Ping)

My name is Jeff. Her name is Annie. We are both foreign students. Our teacher's last name is Tian.

Lesson Five   Which class are you in?

（一）

(On the way)

Peter:　　Good morning!
Annie:　　Morning!
Peter:　　What's your name?
Annie:　　My name is Annie. And yours?
Peter:　　My name is Peter. Where are you from?
Annie:　　I'm American. Are you American as well?
Peter:　　No. I'm French.

(二)

(Peter comes over)

Annie: Hello Jeff!
Jeff: Hello Annie! Who is this?
Annie: His name is Peter. He is a French.
Jeff: Hello, Peter! My name is Jeff!
Peter: Hello! Are you a British?
Jeff: Yes, I am. May I ask how old you are?
Peter: I am nineteen. And you?
Jeff: I'm twenty. Which class are you in?
Peter: Class one. And you?
Annie: I'm in class two.
Jeff: I am in class two as well.

(三)

(Peter says)

I'm French. I'm nineteen years old. Annie is an American. Jeff is a British. I'm in class 1. Both of them are in Class 2.

Lesson Six What time is it now?

(一)

(Morning, in the dormitory)

Annie: Lisa, what time is it now?
Lisa: It's seven thirty.
Annie: What day of the week is it today?
Lisa: Today is Tuesday.
Annie: I don't have a class at eight o'clock today.

(二)

(Break during class)

Peter: Annie, do you have any classes tomorrow?
Annie: Yes I do.
Peter: What time is your class?
Annie: I have an Oral Chinese lesson from eight to nine fifty in the morning. What about you?
Peter: I don't have any classes tomorrow morning.
Annie: What time is it now?
Peter: Two minutes to nine.
Annie: It's time to go to class now. Bye.
Peter: Bye.

(三)

(Annie says)

　　Today is Tuesday. I don't have any classes at eight o'clock. Tomorrow morning I have an Oral Chinese lesson from eight to nine fifty.

Lesson Seven Where is the dining hall?

(一)

(At the teaching building)

Annie:　　　　Excuse me, is this the classroom of class 3?

Piao Zhiyong: Yes, it's right here.
Annie: Thank you.
Piao Zhiyong: You are welcome.

(二)

Yamada: Excuse me, could you tell me where the dining hall for foreign students is?
A student: It's over there.
Yamada: Over where?
A student: Beside the foreign students' dormitory.
Yamada: Thank you.

(三)

(At the teading building)
A student: Excuse me, where is the washroom?
Jeff: To the right of this classroom ... oh, no. To the left of that classroom.
A student: Thank you.
Jeff: You're welcome.

(四)

(Jeff says)

This is our school. It has a very large campus. This is where we have lessons and that is the foreign student dormitory. The dining hall is beside the dormitory.

Lesson Eight　How much is it all together?

(一)

(In the overseas students' cafeteria)
Attendant: Which dish would you like?
Lisa: I'd like this one. How much is it?
Attendant: Seven yuan fifty fen.
Yamada: I want this one, and that one, too.
Attendant: Which one?
Yamada: The one over there! How much is it all together?
Attendant: Fifteen yuan forty fen.

(二)

(At the shop)
Jeff: I want this kind of bicycle. Which color do you think is better?
Annie: How about the black one?
Jeff: Is the black one good? ...I like blue.
Annie: Excuse me. Do you have this bike in blue?
Salesman: Which one?
Jeff: This one.
Salesman: Yes. We have that in both blue and black.
Jeff: I'll take the blue one. How much is it?
Salesman: Three hundred and forty yuan.

(三)

(Jeff says)

I wanted to buy a bicycle. I took a look at a black one, and a blue one too. I don't like the black one, but I do like the blue one. I paid 340 yuan for the blue bicycle.

Lesson Nine What do you want to do?

(一)

(In Annie's dormitory)

Annie: Jeff, I have a question on today's homework. Can you help me?
Jeff: I do not understand this question, either.
Annie: Shall we ask the teacher?
Jeff: Do you know Ms. Tian's telephone number?
Annie: Yes, I do. Her office number is 64752018.
Jeff: Let me call her now. *(Jeff made a phone call)*
Annie: Is Ms. Tian there?
Jeff: *(Put down the telephone)* She is not there.

(二)

(Jeff gives Wang Ping a call)

Jeff: Hello, May I talk to Wang Ping, please?
Wang Ping: This is Wang Ping speaking.
Jeff: Hello Wang Ping, this is Jeff. Are you free tomorrow night?
Wang Ping: Yes I am. What do you want to do?
Jeff: Tomorrow is my birthday. Let's go out together.
Wang Ping: Ok. Where and when?
Jeff: Six thirty, tomorrow night, in my dormitory building.
Wang Ping: Where do you live?
Jeff: Building 8, room 601.

(三)

(Wang Ping says)

　　Jeff made a call today and told me that tomorrow is his birthday. I'm going to buy him a gift to wish him a happy birthday.

Lesson Ten She is sick

(一)

(Before class)

Lisa: Annie, is something wrong?
Annie: I have a headache.
Lisa: Do you have a cold?
Annie: I think so. I want to go back to my room and get some rest. Could you tell the teacher please?
Lisa: Sure.

(二)

(After class)

Lisa: Ms. Tian, Annie can't come to class today.
Ms. Tian: What's wrong?
Lisa: She was sick. She had a cold.
Ms. Tian: Oh, I see.

(三)

(A half-hour after class, Jeff knocks on the door)

Ms. Tian: Please come in!
Jeff: Sorry I'm late!

(Jeff sits down and Lisa asks in a whisper)

Lisa: Why are you late?

Jeff: Well, my alarm clock "fell asleep," and I didn't wake up until 8:15am. So ...

Lisa: What? Your alarm clock "fell asleep?" Oh! I understand, your alarm clock is broken!

Ms. Tian: *(Look at the two chatting students)* Are there any problems for you two?

Jeff: No, no. Sorry.

(四)

(After class, Lisa asks for a leave)

    Ms. Tian, I have to go to the embassy tomorrow and won't be able to come to class. I want to ask for a half-day leave.

Lesson Eleven　I like tea

(一)

(Dinner time)

Jeff: What do you like to eat?

Annie: I like to eat steamed rolls. What about you?

Jeff: I prefer dumplings. I will order half a jin of dumplings.

Annie: How many dumplings are there in half a jin of dumplings?

Jeff: Maybe thirty.

Annie: Can you eat them all?

Jeff: No problem. They made delicious dumplings here.

(二)

(In a small shop)

Annie: Are these grapes sour?

Shop assistant: No. They're sweet.

Annie: May I taste one?

Shop assistant: Sure, you can try one. You don't need to buy them if they aren't sweet.

(Annie tasted a grape)

Annie: They are very good! How much for one jin?

Shop assistant: Four yuan fifty fen.

Annie: Can you give me a cheaper price?

Shop assistant: Sorry, we can't bargain here.

Annie: OK, I will buy a jin.

(三)

(Jeff and Annie go to Peter' dormitory)

Jeff: Hello! Oh, Wang Ping, you're here too!

Wang Ping: Oh, it's you two!

Peter: Welcome! Welcome! Please sit down.

Annie: Ok, Jeff, you sit over there, and I'll sit here.

Peter: What would you like, tea or coffee?

Jeff: Coffee. I like coffee.

Wang Ping: Annie, you like coffee too, don't you?

Annie: No, but I did before.

Wang Ping: And now?

Annie: Now I like tea.

Peter: Annie. Here is your tea. The snack is on the table, enjoy yourself.

Annie: Thanks!

(四)

(Annie says)

  I used to like coffee when I was in America. But since come to China, I got used to drinking tea and now I really like Chinese tea.

Lesson Twelve   What are you doing?

(一)

(Outside Annie's dormitory, Jeff knocks on the door)

Jeff: Is Annie there?
Annie: Door is open, please come in! Jeff, it is you, be seated.
Jeff: Thanks! What's the matter with you? You don't look very happy.
Annie: I am a little homesick.
Jeff: You're homesick? Would you like to listen to some music?
Annie: Ok, let's listen to some music and talk.

(二)

(At the entrance to Jeff's dormitory)

Lisa: Jeff! Jeff!
Jeff: Who is it? Come in!
Lisa: What are you doing?
Jeff: Do my homework! We will have a dictation tomorrow as our teacher said.
Lisa: Can you do your homework well while listening to music?
Jeff: Of course, I can.
Lisa: Really? I have a question to ask. Can you give me the correct answer to my question?
Jeff: No problem! just Ask!

(三)

(Jeff says to Peter)

  Yesterday was Sunday. I went to Annie's room. I noticed that she wasn't very happy. I asked her why and she said she was homesick. I said let's listen to some music. So we listened to some music and chatted for a while and we both felt happy.

(四)

(Jeff says to Lisa)

  I have the habit of doing my exercises while listening to music. My friends said it is not a good habit, but I don't think it is a problem.

Lesson Thirteen   I'm going to the library to borrow books

(一)

(At the entrance to the dormitory)

Annie: Hi, Jeff, where are you going?
Jeff: I'm going to the library to borrow a book.
Annie: I also want to borrow an English book.
Jeff: If you have time now, come with me.
Annie: Sounds good! What time does the library close?
Jeff: After 5:30 in the afternoon there's no borrowing books, but you can still self-study there. The library doesn't close until 10pm at night.

(二)

(Annie says)

　　Yesterday I went to the library to borrow an English book, but they didn't have the book I wanted. Jeff says if I am in a rush, I can buy the book online. Buying things on the internet is so convenient now, and the price is also very cheap. Yesterday afternoon Jeff helped me order online, this morning the book was delivered to my dormitory, so fast!

(三)

(An *Express delivery courier* comes to Lisa's dormitory)

Clerk:	Hello! Do you want to make an express delivery?
Lisa:	Yes, I want to send an express delivery.
Clerk:	Where do you want to deliver?
Lisa:	This book is to be delivered to Shanghai, the clothes to Xi'an.
Clerk:	Please fill out this express delivery form.
Lisa:	Okay. Let me ask you, can the recipient make the payment?
Clerk:	Of course. Both items the recipient will pay for?
Lisa:	The one that goes to Shanghai the recipient will pay, I will pay for the other. The express waybill was done, how much?
Clerk:	Twelve yuan.
Lisa:	Here is fifteen yuan.
Clerk:	Your change is three yuan.

(四)

(Lisa leaves a message on the phone for her friend in Shanghai)

　　Hi, It's Lisa, I have just delivered the book you wanted, it's pay on delivery, please receive it.

Lesson Fourteen   What's the weather like today?

(一)

(Morning, Peter comes back from somewhere)

Jeff:	What's the weather like today?
Peter:	Oh, it's pretty good.
Jeff:	Is it hot?
Peter:	Not very hot. It was drizzling last night.
Jeff:	Is it windy?
Peter:	Not at all.

(二)

(Annie and Wang Ping discuss the weather)

Annie:	Is winter cold here?
Wang Ping:	Yes, quite cold.
Annie:	Are they windy?
Wang Ping:	Very windy.
Annie:	What's the summer like?
Wang Ping:	Extremely hot.
Annie:	How about Spring and Autumn?
Wang Ping:	They are both nice.

(三)

(Li Wenjing Mom's friend Auntie Wang comes)

Li Wenjing:	Aunt Wang, what brings you here?
Aunt Wang:	I heard that you were sick, so I came to see you. How did you get sick?
Li Wenjing:	I'm not used to the climate here, so I got a cold.
Aunt Wang:	How are you feeling now?

Li Wenjing:	I'm all right now.
Aunt Wang:	Are you busy with studying recently?
Li Wenjing:	Not really.
Aunt Wang:	Is the food good in the dining hall?
Li Wenjing:	It's OK.

(四)
(Li Wenjing says)

Aunt Wang, I'm so glad that you came to see me. Please tell my mother that it's very cold and windy here during the winter. Because I am still not very used to the climate here, I got a cold. Please let my mother know that I'm fine now, and I haven't been very busy, so she doesn't need to worry.

Lesson Fifteen   How many class hours are there in a week?

(一)
(Break during class)

Jeff:	Annie, when do we start winter vacation?
Annie:	January 15th.
Jeff:	When is the final exam?
Annie:	At the beginning of the semester, the teacher said it should be from January 8th to January 14th.
Jeff:	Do we have holidays for Christmas?
Annie:	No, I don't think so.
Jeff:	How long will the winter vacation be?
Annie:	Probably a month.

(二)
(On the way to classroom)

Piao Zhiyong:	Annie, are you going to class?
Annie:	Uh-huh!
Piao Zhiyong:	How many courses are you taking this term?
Annie:	Three. A Grammar class, an oral class, and a listening comprehension class. How many are you taking?
Piao Zhiyong:	I have four classes.
Annie:	How many lessons do you have each week?
Piao Zhiyong:	20 lessons. I have eight lessons of Chinese grammar and spoken Chinese. There are two lessons for listening comprehension and two lessons for Chinese characters as well.
Annie:	How many lessons do you have today?
Piao Zhiyong:	Four: two in the morning and two in the afternoon.

(三)
(Piao Zhiyong says)

I am in class 3, Annie is in class 2. I take four courses, and she takes three. We both have 20 lessons every week. There are too many students in my class—17, and there are less students in her class—12.

(四)
(Teacher Tian explains)

There are two semesters in the school year. The first term lasts 19 weeks, starting in September and ending in January of next year. The second term lasts 18 weeks; it starts in February and ends in July. There is a winter vacation and a summer vacation as well.

Lesson Sixteen   Could you show me the way to the zoo?

(一)

(In the shopping mall)

Peter: Excuse me, where can I buy some shoes?
Clerk: At the third floor, on the right side.
Peter: Thank you.
Clerk: No problem.

(二)

(On the road)

Annie: Sir, could you show me the way to the zoo, please?
A Passer-by: If you go straight, it's on the left side of the street.
Annie: Is it far?
A Passer-by: No. It's just a couple of minutes walk.
Annie: Thank you.
A Passer-by: You are welcome.

(三)

(In the school hospital)

Jeff: Excuse me, where is the Dentistry Department, please?
A student: Well, I'm not sure. Maybe it's at the second floor. You should ask someone else.

(Jeff goes to the second floor)

Jeff: Excuse me, Doctor. Is the Dentistry Department on this floor?
Doctor: Yes, keep going, turn right and it's the second door on the left.
Jeff: Thank you very much.

(四)

(Jeff tells Annie)

These days my teeth are very painful. I went to the hospital to see the dentist after class yesterday, but I didn't know where the Dentistry Department is. I found it after asking two people for directions. It is at the second floor. I went upstairs, walked straight and turned right. It is the second door on the left-handside.

Lesson Seventeen   Tasty as well as inexpensive

(一)

(In a restaurant)

Server: Welcome! How many people are there?
Jeff: Three people.
Server: Please come in.

(After the three persons sit down)

Jeff: What food do you like?
Annie: We like sweet and sour food.
Jeff: How about you, Lisa?
Lisa: I like spicy food.
Jeff: Waiter! Order food!
Waiter: Hello! Here is the menu, what do you want to eat?
Jeff: Which dishes are sweet and sour?
Waiter: There's sweet and sour fish, tomato and scrambled egg...

Annie:	I don't really like to eat fish, how about the tomato and scrambled egg?
Lisa:	Ok. I want a fish-flavored eggplant.
Jeff:	Fish and eggplant? Annie said she doesn't like fish.
Lisa:	Don't worry, there's no fish in fish-flavored eggplant, "fish-flavor" is only a kind of flavor.
Jeff:	What flavor is it?
Lisa:	I really can't say for sure, when you eat it in a moment, you'll know.
Jeff:	Alright. I'll order a meat-dish, give us a sizzling beef, also fried potato shreds. Are four dishes enough?
Annie:	That's enough.
Lisa:	Give us three bowls of white rice.
Waiter:	What would you like to drink?
Jeff:	Two bottles of beer. We're very hungry, make it quick, ok?
Waiter:	Ok, it will come right away.

(二)

(After an hour)

Annie:	Lisa, how about the dishes in this restaurant?
Lisa:	The dishes here are much more delicious than those in the canteen.
Jeff:	Are you full?
Annie:	Too full. You can eat more.
Jeff:	I'm also full. Let's take-away the food we haven't finished. Waiter! Pay the bill!

(三)

(Jeff says to Peter)

Annie, Lisa, and I went and ate at a restaurant yesterday. We ordered four dishes and they all were delicious. I think the dishes in the restaurant are tasty as well as inexpensive.

Lesson Eighteen   Will you be my tutor?

(一)

Annie:	Have you been busy lately?
Wang Ping:	Not very, why?
Annie:	Would you mind being my tutor?
Wang Ping:	I wouldn't mind at all. What tutorials do you need?
Annie:	Well, I want to practice my spoken Chinese twice a week for an hour. Is that okay?
Wang Ping:	No problem! What time is most suitable for you?
Annie:	How about every Monday and Thursday afternoon, from 5:00 to 6:00?
Wang Ping:	I have class on Monday afternoon. Is Thursday all right?
Annie:	Ok. How much is it for an hour?
Wang Ping:	It is free for you.
Annie:	No, that's not acceptable!
Wang Ping:	How about this idea? You help me practice spoken English when you have time.
Annie:	That sounds terrific. Let's exchange our knowledge!

(二)

(Annie says to Jeff)

I cannot speak Chinese well, especially my pronunciation, so I asked Wang Ping to be my tutor. I expect to be tutored twice a week, for an hour every time. Wang Ping has gladly approved. Starting from next week, every Tuesday and Thursday afternoon, he will tutor me in Chinese for an hour and I will tutor him in English for another hour.

(三)

(In the classroom)

Jeff: Annie, Wang Ping was just in a hurry looking for you, but you weren't here, and your phone was off.
Annie: I was just in class. Did he say anything?
Jeff: He said this afternoon's tutoring was cancelled, he has to go to see a friend.
Annie: I see. Thank you.
Jeff: How are his tutorials?
Annie: Pretty good.
Jeff: What do you talk about?
Annie: Hobbies, travelling, career, and so on.
Jeff: That must be very interesting. Can I join in next time?
Annie: Sure, you are welcome to join us.

Lesson Nineteen   I don't feel very well

(一)

(Break during class)

Zhang Xin: Excuse me, Miss, I don't feel very well. May I go back to my room and have a rest?
Teacher: What's the matter?
Zhang Xin: Well, I have a bad headache, and seem like I have a fever too.
Teacher: All right, take a good rest and drink more water. Go to see a doctor if you have a fever.
Zhang Xin: Thank you, Miss.

(二)

(After class)

Yamada: Annie, did you have a test?
Annie: We did, last Friday.
Yamada: Well, how was it? Did you do well?
Annie: No. I didn't feel well last week and didn't have enough time to prepare for it.
Yamada: It's all right, you can prepare well for the next test.

(三)

(Annie says to Yamada)

   We had a test last Friday. But I had a cold, cough a lot plus had a running nose, just two days before the exam and didn't have much time to prepare for the test. I got a bad headache during the test as well. That was why I didn't do very well. I'll try harder to prepare well next time.

(四)

(In the dormitory)

Li Wenjing: Zhang Xin, I heard you got sick. Are you feeling better now?
Zhang Xin: Thanks for your concern. I caught a bad cold several days ago, I feel much better now.
Li Wenjing: Well, it is so nice. I'd like to go out for a walk, would you?
Zhang Xin: I'm sorry I can't. A friend is coming to see me soon.
Li Wenjing: Who? Is it your boyfriend?
Zhang Xin: No, don't joke.
Li Wenjing: Well, I will go now. See you later.
Zhang Xin: Thanks again. See you and take care.

Lesson Twenty What is your hobby?

(一)
(Dinner time)

Jeff: What do you do every evening?
Lisa: I do my assignments, listen to the tapes, and review old lessons, study new lessons in advance...
Jeff: You're really a good student.
Lisa: Well, what do you usually do in the evening?
Jeff: Watch television and chat with friends.
Lisa: I enjoy chatting as well.
Jeff: You don't like watching television, do you?
Lisa: No, I don't like watching Chinese TV.
Jeff: Why not?
Lisa: The language used on TV is beyond my comprehension.

(二)
(Outside of the dormitory building)

Annie: What would you like to do this weekend?
Yamada: Go mountain climbing. There is a wonderful mountain to the west of here. Shall we go together?
Annie: Sorry, I can't.
Yamada: Why? You don't like mountain climbing?
Annie: Climbing Mountains is too tiring. I enjoy window-shopping more.
Yamada: Well, I think window-shopping is even more tiring than climbing mountains is!

(三)
(During tutoring)

Annie: Wang Ping, what are your interests?
Wang Ping: I like sports, especially ping-pong.
Annie: Do you play ping-pong often?
Wang Ping: I have joined the school team and play ping-pong almost every weekend.
Annie: I don't play ping-pong at all. Is it difficult to learn?
Wang Ping: No, it's not difficult.

(四)
(Lisa says to Annie)

Jeff likes watching television and chatting. I like chatting too, but I don't really like watching Chinese television programs because the language is beyond my comprehension.

(五)
(Annie says to Lisa)

Yamada likes to spend his weekends climbing mountains. I think climbing mountains is too tiring. I enjoy window-shopping. But Yamada says window-shopping is even more tiring than climbing mountains is.

Lesson Twenty One At eight I'm in class

(一)
(Liu Wei comes to Zhang Xin's dormitory)

Zhang Xin: Liu Wei, what are you doing here? Why didn't you call first?
Liu Wei: I called a few times, but you didn't answer.
Zhang Xin: Really? How did I not hear it? Let me see. Oh, I'm really sorry, my cell phone was out of juice, and I forgot to charge it.

Liu Wei:	Last night I also called.
Zhang Xin:	What time did you call?
Liu Wei:	Around eight.
Zhang Xin:	At eight I'm in class.
Liu Wei:	Yesterday was Sunday, what class was it?
Zhang Xin:	Calligraphy class.
Liu Wei:	When did you start studying calligraphy?
Zhang Xin:	I started it half a year ago. Did you come to see me for something?
Liu Wei:	I have two tickets for a movie tonight, my friend gave them to me. I want to invite you to go with me. Do you have time?
Zhang Xin:	Thank you, but tonight I have already appointed to have dinner to eat with a friend.
Liu Wei:	No problem, then I'll find someone else to go.

(二)

(During tutoring)

Wang Ping:	Annie, you have made a great progress in your Chinese recently.
Annie:	Really? But I have a big problem now.
Wang Ping:	What is the problem?
Annie:	I don't recognize many Chinese characters in the textbook. moreover, I can't write them either. What should I do?
Wang Ping:	I have a good idea.
Annie:	What's your idea? Please tell me!
Wang Ping:	There's no hurry, listen to me. You could practice Chinese calligraphy with me, couldn't you?
Annie:	Calligraphy? It is too hard, I'm afraid I am not able to do it!
Wang Ping:	Take it easy. The more reading and writing you do, the better your calligraphy is.
Annie:	Ok, if I write down five characters a day, I might be able to learn more than five hundred characters in a semester!
Wang Ping:	In addition, don't only rely on the pinyin when you read your book.

(三)

(Annie says)

My big problem is that I don't recognize many characters when learning Chinese. I asked Wang Ping what I should do. Wang Ping suggested that I practice Chinese calligraphy with him. He also told me not to rely solely on the pinyin when I read my textbook. I think I will learn Chinese faster and better if I concentrate on writing and reading.

Lesson Twenty Two   We came back from travelling

(一)

Annie:	Jeff, it's almost the weekend. What do you plan to do this weekend?
Jeff:	I'm going on a trip.
Annie:	Where?
Jeff:	It is not far from here. It is a nice place with hills and waters.
Annie:	Are you going alone?
Jeff:	I've asked Wang Ping, two of us will go together.
Annie:	I don't have any arrangements yet for the weekend. Can I go with you?
Jeff:	Certainly!

(二)

(In the dormitory)

Lisa:	Annie, are you back from vacations? Well, did you have fun?
Annie:	We had great fun.

Lisa:	Tired?
Annie:	It was a bit tiring.
Lisa:	You haven't had supper yet, have you? Let's have supper together.
Annie:	I want to take a bath first before supper.
Lisa:	OK, I'll wait for you. But you must hurry up, the dining hall will be closing soon!

(三)

(Annie says to Lisa)

Jeff, Wang Ping and I went on vacations this weekend. We went to a beautiful place. There are many hills and beautiful waters. It's probably more than 10 kilometers from our school. We rode bikes there, and we had great fun when we were riding and singing. I'm going to take a bath now, and then we will have supper together. Please wait for me.

(四)

(Wang Ping is sipping soup in a restaurant, Annie and Lisa enter)

Wang Ping:	Ladies, why are you eating here, too?
Lisa:	Well, the dining hall was closed. So we are going to enjoy ourselves and go out to eat.
Annie:	Have you just be here too, Wang Ping? Let's eat together.
Wang Ping:	Oh no, I am almost finished.
Lisa:	Aren't you having your soup? A bowl of soup is enough for you?
Wang Ping:	(laugh heartily) You think the soup is served first in a Chinese restaurant, don't you?
Lisa:	Don't laugh at us, please. We don't really know all the rules for eating a Chinese meal. I would be delightful if you told us about them.
Wang Ping:	Ok, let me tell you then. In a Chinese restaurant, usually cold dishes are served first. Drink while eating cold dishes, after a while, eat the hot dishes and rice. The soup is served later, sometimes followed simply by the last course, the fruit.

Lesson Twenty Three   What shall I wear?

(一)

(In the dormitory)

Annie:	I wonder if it's cold outside today. What shall I wear?
Lisa:	The weather forecast says it's a bit colder than yesterday.
Annie:	Is it? But it looks like there's a bit sunshine outside.
Lisa:	I have just come back from outside, it's rather cold. Put on your overcoat if you go out.

(二)

(On the way to class)

Li Wenjing:	Jeff, aren't you cold wearing so little?
Jeff:	So little? Well, I don't think I'm wearing too little. These are my warmest clothes.
Li Wenjing:	Winter is getting near. You'll have to buy a heavier overcoat.
Jeff:	It won't be necessary, will it? It's said the winter here is not too cold.
Li Wenjing:	Here is very windy. You have to wear a down filled coat in winter.
Jeff:	Is that so? Ok, I'll get one this weekend. If you have time, would you mind coming with me and helping me choose one?

(三)

(In the shopping mall)

Li Wenjing:	What about this one?
Jeff:	The style is all right, but I don't like the color.
Li Wenjing:	How about that one? The one on the right.

Jeff:	It's not bad. *(Talk to the shop assistant)* I'd like to have a look at that one, may I try it on?
shop assistant:	Yes. There's a mirror over there.

(Jeff tries on clothing)

Jeff:	Oh, it's so tight and short, it's much too small.
Li Wenjing:	It's not because the coat is too short and small, but that you are too tall.

(Talk to the shop assistant)

Excuse me, do you have this coat in a large size?

Shop assistanrt:	*(Find one after a while)* This is the biggest one, Mister, please try it again.
Li Wenjing:	This one is longer than that one, as well as fatter.

(After trying)

Jeff:	It is still not suitable. Forget it, I will buy it when I "grow small".
Li Wenjing:	Let's go shopping somewhere else.

(四)

(Jeff says to Peter)

    Winter is coming. It's getting colder day by day. I didn't bring a warm overcoat for winter. Yesterday, Li Wenjing accompanied me for shopping, bought a down filled coat. I tried on some, but was unable to find one that suits me.

Lesson Twenty Four   How many people are there in your family?

(一)

Annie:	Wang Ping, what are you planning to do after graduation next year?
Wang Ping:	I want to study in United States.
Annie:	If you go to study in the United States, you can visit my family and have fun.
Wang Ping:	Oh, how wonderful. What do your parents do?
Annie:	Well, my father is a lawyer and my mother is a doctor.
Wang Ping:	Are there any other members of your family?
Annie:	I have an elder brother and a younger sister.
Wang Ping:	Are they both at home?
Annie:	My sister is in high school. She lives at home. My brother is in college. He comes home only at the weekends.
Wang Ping:	Would they welcome me?
Annie:	Of course they would! They are all very warm-hearted.

(二)

(Annie says to Wang Ping)

    If you go to graduate schools in America, you can visit my family. There are five people in my family. My father is a lawyer and my mother is a doctor. I have an elder brother and a younger sister. My brother is a college student and my sister is a high school student. I'm sure that you will be very much welcome in my family.

(三)

(In Lisa's dormitory)

Peter:	Lisa, is this your photo? May I have a look?
Lisa:	Sure.
Peter:	Is this a photo of your family?
Lisa:	Yes! Is it wonderful?

Peter:	Terrific! Which one are you?
Lisa:	Well, you can find it out!
Peter:	Oh, both of the girls in the picture look alike ... ... You are the one in red at the back, right?
Lisa:	No, that is my sister.
Peter:	So you are the one in the front! You two look very much alike.

Lesson Twenty Five   How do you intend to spend the winter vocation?

(一)

Li Wenjing:	Annie, this semester's almost over, how do you intend to spend the winter vacation?
Annie:	As soon as vacation starts, I will go back to my country.
Li Wenjing:	In such a rush!
Annie:	I miss my family too much!
Li Wenjing:	Next semester will you still study here?
Annie:	I'll be here, I already applied for a half-year extension. How about you, where will you go for vacation?
Li Wenjing:	Of course I will go back to my hometown to celebrate Spring Festival.
Annie:	Next week is New Year Day, we're having an evening gala to celebrate, you can also join in us.
Li Wenjing:	Sounds good. What do I need to prepare?
Annie:	You don't need to prepare anything. If it's convenient, bring something to eat or drink, anything's fine.

(二)

Lisa:	Jeff, next week we finish exams, what day are you going back to your country?
Jeff:	I'm not going back. I will travel in China.
Lisa:	Where to?
Jeff:	I haven't made my final decision, I want to go to several places.
Lisa:	You should hurry up and decide.
Jeff:	Why?
Lisa:	I heard that a lot of Chinese people head home for Spring Festival, a lot of people also go travelling, so plane tickets and train tickets are hard to get. If you don't reserve a ticket early, you might not be able to buy it.
Jeff:	Is that so? Thanks for telling me this. As soon as I get back to my dorm, I'm will get online and search for the best place to go.

(三)

(Jeff Says)

Winter vacation is coming. Annie is going back to her country, I intend to travel to the south. I already reserved a plane ticket to go to Kunming on the tenth of January. Yunnan has a lot of fun places, I intend to spend around ten days there and then go to Hainan. Hope everybody has a good vacation!

练习参考答案

第三课

二、yì mǐ　　yì zhāng　　yí gòng　　yí xià　　yì pán　　yí lù
yì běn　　yí huìr　　bù suān　　bù míngbai　　bù xiǎo
bú kuài　　bú guì　　bù néng　　bú cuò　　bú dà

三、ī→(yī)　　ǔ→(wǔ)　　ǚ→(yǔ)　　iá→(yá)
uǒ→(wǒ)　　üè→(yuè)　　iǎn→(yǎn)　　uā→(wā)
üǎn→(yuǎn)　　iào→(yào)　　uài→(wài)　　ún→(yún)
iǒu→(yǒu)　　uéi→(wéi)　　jǔ→(jǔ)　　īn→(yīn)
ùen→(wèn)　　qù→(qù)　　íng→(yíng)　　uàn→(wàn)
xǔ→(xū)　　iòng→(yòng)　　uàng→(wàng)　　xuǎn→(xuǎn)

第四课

四、1. 你好!　　2. 我叫杰夫。
3. 我叫安妮。　　4. 我们是留学生。我叫安妮,他叫杰夫。

五、1. 你叫什么名字?　　2. 你姓什么?／我姓田,你呢?　　3. 我是中国人,你呢?

第五课

一、4. 一班 yī bān　　他们 tāmen　　美国 Měiguó
留学生 liúxuéshēng　　什么 shénme　　老师 lǎoshī
我们 wǒmen　　名字 míngzi

四、1. 对,我是。　　2. 他是我的老师。　　3. 我二十岁。　　4. 三班。

五、1. 早上好!　　2. 你是哪国人?　　3. 你是中国人吗?
4. 你多大?　　5. 我在二班,你呢?

第六课

一、4. 几点 jǐ diǎn　　今天 jīntiān　　上课 shàng kè　　口语课 kǒuyǔkè
明天 míngtiān　　再见 zàijiàn　　哪国人 nǎ guó rén　　七点半 qī diǎn bàn

六、1. 两点。　　2. 星期二。　　3. 没有课。

第七课

一、4. 请问 qǐngwèn　　右边 yòubian　　厕所 cèsuǒ　　左边 zuǒbian
旁边 pángbiān　　教室 jiàoshì　　学校 xuéxiào　　地方 dìfang

五、1. 在这儿。　　2. 不用谢!　　3. 很大。　　4. 在左边。

六、

A	B
谢谢!	在那个教室的旁边。
请问,厕所在哪儿?	我是中国人。
你是哪国人?	不用谢!
早上好!	对,我是从美国来的。
你叫什么名字?	我二十一岁。
你是留学生吗?	早上好!
你今年多大?	不,在那儿。
请问,留学生食堂在这儿吗?	我叫安妮。

第八课

一、4. 喜欢 xǐhuan　　　黑色 hēisè　　　一共 yígòng　　　怎么样 zěnmeyàng

八、1. 你要哪件衣服？　　2. 这本书多少钱？　　3. 这辆车怎么样？
　　4. 这种鞋有蓝的吗？　　5. 你买这件衣服花了多少钱？

第九课

一、4. 问题 wèntí　　知道 zhīdào　　快乐 kuàilè　　有时间 yǒu shíjiān

六、1. 老师说今天没有作业。/今天老师说没有作业。
　　2. 上午老师给我打了电话。/老师上午给我打了电话。
　　3. 他给我买了一件礼物。
　　4. 星期天晚上你有时间吗？/你星期天晚上有时间吗？
　　5. 明天八点在一班的教室上课。

七、1. 甲：今天有时间吗？　　　　　　乙：没时间。
　　　甲：现在几点？　　　　　　　　乙：不知道。
　　　甲：什么时候有时间？　　　　　乙：明天。
　　　甲：明天我去你的宿舍，好吗？　乙：三点。
　　　甲：几点上课？　　　　　　　　乙：好。
　　　　　　　　　　　　　　　　　　乙：两点。

　　2. 甲：你有时间吗？　　　　　　　乙：什么事？
　　　甲：我要去王平的宿舍，你去吗？乙：今天。
　　　甲：我去上课。　　　　　　　　乙：对不起，我现在没有时间。
　　　乙：一起去吧。
　　　甲：昨天*呢？　　　　　　　　　乙：我不懂。
　　　甲：明天呢？　　　　　　　　　乙：也没有时间。
　　　甲：好。
　　　甲：你真*忙*！

第十课

一、4. 怎么 zěnme　　　告诉 gàosu　　　请假 qǐng jià　　　大使馆 dàshǐguǎn

五、1. 我头很疼。　　2. 我没感冒。　　3. 好吧。
　　4. 是。　　　　　5. 没关系，不晚。

第十一课

一、4. 大概 dàgài　　　葡萄 pútao　　　便宜 piányi
　　　以前 yǐqián　　　习惯 xíguàn

五、1. 大概五百个。　　2. 没问题。　　3. 不行。

八、来中国 以前，我不 喜欢 喝茶，我喜欢喝咖啡。来中国 以后，我也 习惯 喝茶了。我觉得茶 很 好喝，我每天都喝很多茶。

第十二课

一、4. 当然 dāngrán　　回答 huídá　　高兴 gāoxìng　　有点儿 yǒudiǎnr

五、1. 谢谢！　　2. 好。　　3. 当然可以。　　4. 真的。

六、1. 他怎么了？　2. 你喝咖啡吗？　3. 你们干什么呢？　4. 谁啊？什么事？
　　5. 她怎么了？好像不太高兴？

第十三课

一、4. 关门 guān mén　　可以 kěyǐ　　借书 jiè shū　　图书馆 túshūguǎn

第十四课

一、4. 天气 tiānqì　　非常 fēicháng　　听说 tīngshuō　　放心 fàng xīn

第十五课

一、3. 寒假 hánjià　　　语法 yǔfǎ　　　下午 xiàwǔ　　　不放暑假 bú fàng shǔjià

五、1. 一月。　　　2. 昨天吃饭的时候。　　　3. 大概三个小时。　　　4. 三门课。
　　5. 三周。　　　6. 没学过。　　　7. 第二天。

六、1. 你的生日是什么时候？　　　　　　　　2. 你看了多长时间电视？
　　3. 你学了多长时间汉语？　　　　　　　　4. 明天你有几门课？
　　5. 你们一个星期有多少节口语课？　　　　6. 你们学校有多少学生？

八、你有几门课？　　　　　　　　你有多少节课？
　　现在几点？　　　　　　　　　几天？／多长时间？
　　几个小时？／多长时间？　　　多少分钟？／多长时间？
　　几个？　　　　　　　　　　　几月？／什么时候？
　　什么时候？　　　　　　　　　是第一次吗？／第几次？
　　多少钱？　　　　　　　　　　几个月？／多长时间？

第十六课

一、(一) 1. 所以　　马路　　　2. 没有　　练习　　　3. 问题　　身体
　　(二) 1. 咖啡　　冬天　　　　听说
　　　　2. 食堂　　回答　　　　邮局　　　　　　学习
　　　　3. 高兴　　音乐　　　　天气
　　　　4. 旁边　　昨天　　　　明天　　　　　　聊天
　　　　5. 下午　　这里　　　　自己　　　　　　一起

五、1. 三楼。　　　2. 不远。　　　3. 往前走。

第十七课

一、(一) 1. 酸甜　　明天　　　2. 早饭　　学校　　　3. 晚饭　　寒假
　　(二) 1. 阿姨　　喝茶　　　　穿鞋　　　　　　刚才
　　　　2. 天气　　书店　　　　吃饭　　　　　　音乐　　　　听力　　　说话
　　　　3. 菜单　　不高　　　　夏天　　　　　　不听
　　　　4. 觉得　　什么　　　　别的　　　　　　蓝的　　　　回去

五、1. 不吃。　　　2. 三个人。　　　3. 看不懂。　　　　　　4. 不错。

六、1. 你喜欢吃什么味道的菜？
　　2. 吃点儿什么？／你想吃什么菜？／你点(要)什么菜？
　　3. 一碗米饭够吗？／一碗米饭够不够？
　　4. 这个饭馆的菜怎么样？／这个饭馆的菜好吃吗？
　　5. 你吃饱了吗？

第十八课

一、(一) 1. 放心　　第一　　　2. 尝尝　　花钱　　　3. 六楼　　今天
　　(二) 1. 辅导　　手表　　　　早晚　　　　　　左拐　　　　使馆
　　　　2. 练习　　一瓶　　　　去年　　　　　　快来　　　　季节
　　　　3. 答应　　真的　　　　他们　　　　　　休息　　　　衣服
　　　　4. 专业　　吃醋　　　　周末　　　　　　听课

第十九课

一、(一) 1. 努力　　厉害　　　2. 老师　　感冒　　　3. 风雨　　聊天儿
　　(二) 1. 准备　　考试　　　　努力　　　　　　米饭
　　　　　好看　　几岁　　　　礼物　　　　　　点菜
　　　　2. 散步　　下课　　　　教室
　　　　3. 改天　　几天　　　　想家　　　　　　好吃　　　　每天

五、1. 我有点儿不舒服。 2. 比前两天好一点儿。
3. 比前两天好多了。 4. 慢走!

六、1. 1) 有点儿 2) 一点儿 3) 一点儿
     4) 有点儿 一点儿 5) 有点儿 一点儿
   2. 1) 上 2) 上 下 3) 下 4) 下 5) 上 6) 上 7) 上 下
   3. 1) 一会儿 2) 一下儿 3) 一下儿
     4) 一会儿／一下儿 5) 一会儿 6) 一会儿

第二十课

一、(一) 1. 听力 爱好 2. 爬山 旧课 3. 节目 电视
   (二) 1. 特别 预习 复习 季节
        去年 下楼 问题
      2. 参加 乒乓 西山 分钟 今天
      3. 录音 一般 逛街 办公 看书 借书

第二十一课

一、(一) 1. 大概 学期 2. 星期 练习 3. 看看 拼音
   (二) 1. 书法 吃饱 桌椅 喝酒 多远
      2. 认识 路上 要是 地方 病了 客气
      3. 进步 快慢 快乐 汉字 作业 卖票

五、1. 六点来的。 2. 哪里。 3. 别着急,慢慢学。 4. 记不住。

六、1. 王平来北京了吗? 2. 王平是什么时候来的?
   3. 王平是从哪儿来的? 4. 王平是怎么来的?
   5. 王平到北京来干什么?

第二十二课

一、(一) 1. 早上 离开 2. 洗澡 苹果
   (二) 1. 骑车 十八 爬山 滑冰 图书 凉风
      2. 以为 打球 考完 很甜
        起床 旅行 好玩儿
      3. 漂亮 意思 这么 告诉 辣的

五、1. 不一定。 2. 还没打算。 3. 他回家去了。

第二十三课

四、1. 算了。 2. 不错。
   3. 明天不冷,不用穿羽绒服。 4. 有点儿肥。

六、1. 错。 2. 错。 3. 对。 4. 错。 5. 对。

第二十四课

四、1. 没错。 2. 还没呢,明年毕业。
   3. 去年。 4. 她个子很高,长得很漂亮。

五、1. 你家有几口人? 2. 你家有什么人? 3. 你爸爸做什么工作?
   4. 哪个是你的朋友? 5. 请给我们照张照片,好吗?

六、(明年)你大学毕业以后到美国(读/上)研究生的话,可以来我家玩儿。我家有四(口)人,我爸爸是大学老师,妈妈是医生,还有一个弟弟,(正在)上中学。他们都(会)欢迎你的。

八、1. 错。 2. 对。 3. 对。 4. 对。

第二十五课

六、1. 以后 2. 然后 以后